DISTRIBUTED SYSTEMS

by

Garima Verma
Khushboo Saxena
Sandeep Saxena

FIRST EDITION 2015
REPRINT 2017
Copyright © BPB Publications, India

ISBN : 978-81-8333-545-4

Distributors:

BPB PUBLICATIONS
20, Ansari Road, Darya Ganj,
NEW DELHI-110002
Ph: 23254990/23254991

MICRO MEDIA
Shop No. 5, Mahendra Chambers,
150 DN Rd. Next to Capital Cinema,
V.T. (C.S.T.) Station, MUMBAI-400 001
Ph: 22078296/22078297

DECCAN AGENCIES
4-3-329, Bank Street,
HYDERABAD-500195
Ph: 24756967/24756400

COMPUTER BOOK CENTRE 12,
Shrungar Shopping Centre, M.G.
Road, BENGALURU-560001 Ph:
25587923, 25584641

BPB BOOK CENTRE
376, Old Lajpat Rai Market,
DELHI-110 006,
Ph: 23861747

Published by Manish Jain for BPB Publications, 20 Ansari Road, Darya Ganj, New Delhi- 110002 and Printed by him at Repro India Ltd.

Dedicated To

My Parents
Sri. Surendra Mohan Verma, Smt. Nutan Verma

Garima Verma

My Parents
Sri A. P. Saxena, Smt. Manorama Saxena

Khushboo Saxena

My Parents
Sri Keshav Prakash Saxena, Smt. Shobha Kumari Saxena

Sandeep Saxena

Acknowledgement

No one walks alone in the journey of life. The successful implementation of this book involves cooperation and coordination of various peoples at different levels.It is impossible to thank individually but we are here by making humble effort to thanks some of them.

We wish to thank to many of our colleagues and professors across the department of Computer Science & Engineering for their insightful suggestion and knowledge sharing with whom we have been privileged to be associated over the last many years. Whether or not they intended to teach, we have learned a lot from interactions with several of them.

In particular we are grateful to our old school, college teachers and professors, who have introduced us to the sense of Knowledge and Engineering.

We thank our family for their patience and support during this book work and their dedicated editorial suggestions.

We would like to express our sincere feeling of gratitude to the **Dr. Goutam Sanyal** (Senior Professor, NIT Durgapur). They always motivate us to achieve high academic excellence.

We acknowledge the benefit from many of the conversation on Distributed System with our colleagues. In particular Dr. Shashank Srivastava (Assistant Professor, MNNIT, Allahabad), Dr. Arun Sharma (HOD. (CS), KIET,Ghaziabad),Mr. Ashwini Kumar (Galgotias University, Gr. Noida) Mr. Surendra Kesari (KIET, Ghaziabad), Mr. Sansar Singh Chauhan (HOD (CS) Accurate Institute of Management & Technology, Greater Noida),Mr. Sanjeev Pippal and Ms Shraddha Parganiha(JRE, Greater Noida), Mr. S.P.S Chauhan , Mr. Abhishekh Shivhare, (ITS, Greater Noida), Mr. Aditya Saxena (IIIT, Allahabad),Mr. Akhilendra Pratap Singh (NIT, Meghalaya), Mr. Ashutosh Pal (BITS Mesra).

We also thank the Publisher and the whole staff of BPB Publication, especially **Mr. Manish Jain** for bringing this text in a nice presentable form and having faith on us.

Finally, I want to thank everyone who has directly or indirectly contributed to complete this authentic work.

Authors:
Ms. Garima Verma
Ms. Khushboo Saxena
Mr. Sandeep Saxena

Preface

The authors are confident that the present work will come as a relief to the students wishing to go through a comprehensive work explaining difficult concepts in the layman's language, offering a variety of numerical and conceptual problems along with their systematically worked out solutions and to top it, covering all the syllabi prescribed at various levels in universities.

This book promises to be a very good starting point for beginners and an asset to advanced users too.

This book is written as per the syllabus of various Technical Universities of India for the complete coverage of the syllabus for the courses of B.Tech and MCA. Students of B.Sc. (CS), PGDCA, M.Sc. (CS) and DOEACC Society can also use this book .The content of this book are also useful for various polytechnic institutions running this subject. Difficult concepts of Distributed System are given in an easy way, so that students can be able to understand it in an efficient manner.

It is said "To err is human, to forgive divine". In this light we wish that the shortcomings of the book will be forgiven. At the same the authors are open to any kind of constructive criticisms and suggestions for further improvement. All intelligent suggestions are welcome and the authors will try their best to incorporate such in valuable suggestions in the subsequent editions of this book.

Authors:

Garima Verma
Khushboo Saxena
Sandeep Saxena

Table of Content

Unit 1

Chapter 3: Theoretical Foundation 31

Unit 2

Chapter 4: Distributed Mutual Exclusion 53

Unit 3

Unit 5

Unit–I

Characterization of Distributed Systems: Introduction, Examples of distributed Systems, Resource sharing and the Web Challenges. Architectural models, Fundamental Models.

Theoretical Foundation for Distributed System: Limitation of Distributed system, absence of global clock, shared memory, Logical clocks, Lamport's & vectors logical clocks.

Concepts in Message Passing Systems: causal order, total order, total causal order, Techniques for Message Ordering, Causal ordering of messages, global state, termination detection.

Chapter I
Characterization of Distributed System

1.1 Introduction to Distributed System
[UPTU 2008, 10, 12]

A distributed system is composed up of several computers that do not share a common memory or a clock. These computers communicate with each other by passing messages over a communication network and each of these computer run their own operating system and has their own memory.

According to Leslie Lamport

"A distributed system is one that stops you from getting any work done whenever a machine you have never even heard of crashes."

According to Brazier

"A distributed system is a collection autonomous computers linked by a network, with software designed to produce an integrated computing facility."

According to Tanenbaum

"A distributed system is a collection of independent computers that appear to the users of the system as a single computer."

Consequences of Distributed System

Some of the significant consequences for understanding distributed system are as follows:

- **Concurrency:** The convention for any network of computers is its concurrent program execution, which says that the user 'x' will perform its work on his computer and the user 'y' will perform his work on his computer. They are allowed to share resources (such as Web and files) when required. By the addition of more resources (such as computers) to the network, system capacity will be increased for handling shared resources.

- **No Global Clock:** The only way to held communication in a distributed system is by sending messages through the network. It is not possible to have synchronization among multiple computers and does not guarantee to have synchronization over time, therefore events are ordered logically. It is not possible to have a process that could be aware of a single global state.

- **Independent failures:** Whenever faults occur in the network, it results in the isolation of computers, those who are connected to it. But isolating those computers does not mean that they will stop running, this is due to the fact that programs on those computers may not be able to detect that whether the network has failed or it has unusually become slow. In the same manner, unexpected termination of a program or crash (failure) of a computer does not broadcast immediately to the other components with which they communicates.

1.1.1 Requirement of Distributed System [UPTU 2007, 09]

When a group of users are working together they need to communicate with each other, to share data and resources. The requirement of distributed system came from the fact of sharing resources among users. These resources could be hardware (such as disks and printers) or software (such as files, databases and data objects of all kinds).

1.1.2 Advantages and Disadvantages of Distributed System

Some significant advantages of distributed systems are as follows:

- **Resource Sharing:** Whenever a computer requests for a service from another computer, it simply transmits an appropriate request to that computer over a communication network. Such a communication takes place by sharing resources among computers over the network.

- **Enhanced Performance:** Providing rapid response time and higher system throughput is the ability of distributed system and this is mainly because of the fact that many tasks are executed concurrently at different computers. Moreover, to improve the response time, load distributing technique is used by the distributed system. In load distributing technique tasks are transferred from heavily loaded computers to lightly loaded computers.

- **Improved Reliability and Availability:** Improved reliability and availability is provided by distributed system because failure of few components of the system does not affect the availability of the rest of the systems. Distributed system can also be made fault tolerant, through the replication of data and services (processes that provide functionality).

- **Modular Expandability:** New resources either hardware or software can be easily added in a distributed system environment, without replacing it with the existing resources.

Although distributed system have many advantages, they also have some disadvantages, which are as follows:

- **Software:** This is the worst problem for a distributed system. At present, very few software are available for a distributed system, because designing, implementing and using such distributed software is a challenging task till date.

- **Network:** Second problem arises in a distributed system due to its communication network. When two or more devices are communicating, it is possible that they lose messages over communication network, which could be recovered by special software. Using this software could overload the system due to which network saturates. This situation can be handled either by replacing the current network or by adding one more network, both the methods involve great expense.

- **Security:** Security is always a major concern for any environment. Sharing data easily is an advantage but it is also a disadvantage for a distributed system. Because people can very easily access the data (either or their use or not) all over network, which effect the security feature.

1.1.3 Centralized System versus Distributed System

Table 1.1 summarizes the comparison between centralized system and distributed system.

Table 1.1 Comparison between Centralized System and Distributed System

Centralized System	Distributed System
Have non-autonomous components.	Have autonomous components.
This type of system has been often built by using homogeneous technology.	These type of systems may be built by using heterogeneous technology.
Here resources of a centralized system are shared among multiple users all the time.	Distributed system components may be used exclusively and executed in concurrent process.
Have single point of control and failure.	Have multi point failure.

1.1.4 Parallel systems versus Distributed System
[UPTU 2014]

Table 1.2 summarizes the comparison between the parallel system and the distributed system.

Table 1.2: Comparison between Parallel and Distributed System

Parameter	Parallel System	Distributed System
Memory	Tightly-coupled shared memory. memory. For example, UMA (Unified Memory Architecture) and NUMA (Non-Uniform Memory Access).	Message passing, RPC (Remote Procedure Call) and/ or use of distributed shared memory.
Control	Global clock control is needed. For example, SIMD (Single Instruction Multiple Data), MIMD (Multiple Instruction Multiple Data).	No global clock control is required. Synchronization algorithm is required.
Processor Interconnection	Bus, Mesh, Tree, Hypercube network, etc.	(Bus) Ethernet, token ring, and SCI (Serial Communication Interface) (rings), switching network, etc.
Main Focus	Performance computing.	Performance, reliability/ availability,Information/ resource sharing.

Test Your Progress

1. What do you mean by distributed system? Why it is required?
2. Give comparison between distributed system and centralized system.
3. Why is distributed system better than parallel system? Explain.

1.2   Examples of Distributed Systems

The three most widely used and familiar examples of Distributed Systems are as follows:

1. The Internet
2. Intranets
3. Mobile and Ubiquitous computing

1.2.1 Internet

The Internet is a computer network made up of thousands of networks worldwide as shown in Figure 1.1. Interaction among programs running on the computers, (those who are connected to the Internet), held by passing messages. Therefore the major technical achievement is Internet communication mechanism.

The Internet is also considered as a distributed system. Through Internet, users are enabled to use services of World Wide Web (WWW), e-mail, file transfer, etc. Internet Service Providers (ISP's) are the companies which provide modem links and some other types of connection to individual users and small organizations, which enable them to access services anywhere in the Internet. It also provides local services, such as Web hosting and e-mail. For linking the intranets together, backbone is used. A backbone network is a network link with high transmission capacity, which employs satellite connections, fiber optic cables and other high bandwidth circuits.

Multimedia services are also available with the Internet, which enables the users to access audio and video data including video conferences and to hold phone, music, radio and Television channels.

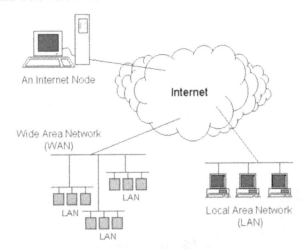

Figure 1.1: Collection of Computer Networks:Internet

1.2.2 Intranet

The portion of Internet that is separately administered is known as an intranet, which has boundary that can be configured to enforce local security policies. Pictorial representation of an intranet is shown in Figure 1.2. Figure illustrates a typical corporate intranet in which A represents firewalls, B represents LANs resources that connect the centrally controlled and managed Local Area Networks (LANs) to the intranet (bridges and routers), C represents the setting done with dial-up Internet access feature for various workstations, and D represents Mainframe access control. The term dial-up Internet access represents a form of Internet access that uses the facilities of the Public Switched Telephone Network (PSTN) to establish a dialed connection to an Internet Service Provider (ISP) via telephone lines.

Where it is composed up of several LAN's (Local Area Networks) connected by a backbone connections.

Router is used to connect the intranet with the Internet, in which the users inside the intranet are allowed to use the services elsewhere, such as World Wide Web (WWW) or e-mail.

Firewall is used to protect an intranet from unauthorized use by malicious users. A firewall can be implemented by incoming messages and outgoing messages. The main issues arise in the designing of components that are used in intranets are:

●   File Services: Needed to enable the user to share data.

- Firewalls with security mechanism is required, when resources are shared among internal and external users.
- Software installation cost and support is an important issue. By using system architectures, such as network computers and their client, cost can be reduced.

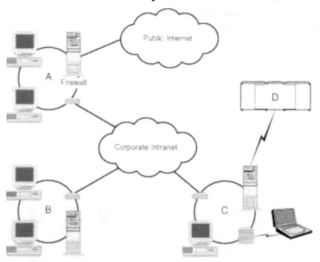

Figure 1.2: An Intranet Setup

1.2.3 Mobile and Ubiquitous Computing

Due to advancement in technology small and portable computing devices are integrated with distributed system (See Figure 1.3). These devices are:

- Laptop computers
- Handheld devices such as, pagers, mobile phones, Personal Digital Assistants (PDA), video and digital cameras, etc.
- Wearable devices, such as smart watches.
- The devices, those who are embedded in appliances, such as wi-fi (Wireless Fidelity) systems, refrigerators, washing machines and cars.

Figure 1.3 represents the portable and handheld devices in a distributed system in which the function of WAP gateway is to sit between mobile devices using the WAP protocol and the World Wide Web (WWW), passing pages from one to the other that works much like a proxy. Wireless application protocol is widely used mobile Internet service which can be used on a handheld device, such as a mobile phone or PDA.

Mobile computing becomes possible because many of these portable devices have the ability to connect with the networks in different places very conveniently. In mobile computing (also known as *nomadic computing* [Kllinrock 1997]) users can access the resources (via portable devices), while they are on move or at visitor's location.

Ubiquitous computing [Weiser 1993], also known as Pervasive computing, is the harnessing of many small cheap computational devices that are present in user's physical environment, such as home, office or elsewhere.

Since mobile user can be benefited from computers that are everywhere, therefore there is overlapping among ubiquitous and mobile computing. But in general, they both are very different. In ubiquitous computing users could get advantage if they remain in a single environment. Whereas in mobile computing users can be profited if only conventional, discrete computers and devices are used.

Use of portable and handheld devices in a distributed system is shown in Figure 1.3, where a user is visiting to a host organization. Here three forms of wireless connection can be accessed by the user, i.e., (1) A laptop is connected to host's wireless LAN, (2) A mobile phone is connected to the Internet using WAP (Wireless Application Proocol) through a gateway. (3) A digital camera is connected to a printer over an infra-red link.

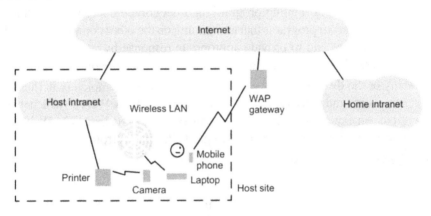

Figure 1.3: Portable and Handheld Devices in a Distributed System

Test Your Progress

1. What is Internet? Illustrate.
2. What is intranet? Write the main issues arise in the designing of components used in the intranet.
3. Give examples of distributed system. Explain them.

1.3   Resource Sharing and the Web   [UPTU 2007, 10]

In a distributed system, resources are:

● Encapsulated within computers.

● They can be accessed from other computers only by communication.

● Can be managed by a program that offers a communication interface.

Resources may be shared in either form (e.g. printer, scanner, etc.) to reduce costs. But the concern of users for sharing resources is to share the higher-level resources that play a part in their application and in their everyday work and social activities.

For example, to share the data in the form of a shared database or a set of Web pages. According to users, shared resources can be a search engine or a currency converter, without regard for the servers that provides these.

In practice, the patterns of resource sharing vary widely depending upon their scope and on how closely users work together. At one extreme, search engine on the Web provides a facility to the users throughout the world, (users who never come in contact with each other directly). At the other extreme, in Computer Supported Cooperative Working (CSCW), the group of users (who cooperate directly), share resources, such as documents in a small closed group. To coordinate user's action, what mechanism must be supplied by the system are determined by the pattern of sharing and the geographic distribution of particular users.

Service is the term used for a distinct part of a computer system that manages a collection of related resources and presents their functionality to the users and application through a well-defined set of operations.

Server, refers to a running program on a networked computer which accepts request messages from programs that are running on the other computers (i.e., client) to perform a service and to provide appropriate response by replying messages. A complete interaction between client and server is called a *remote invocation.*

Many of the distributed systems can be constructed completely in the form of interacting clients and services. For example, the World Wide Web, e-mail, networked printers, etc. An executing Web browser is an example of a client. The Web browser communicates with the Web servers to request Web pages from the server.

Test Your Progress

1. Explain the following terms:

    i.   WWW   ii.   Client

    iii. Server   iv. Remote invocation

    v.   Service

2. Name any six types of hardware or software resources that can be shared efficiently. Also give examples of their sharing as it occurs in distributed system.

1.4   Challenges [UPTU 2008, 09, 10, 14]

Various challenges to build a distributed system are:

1. **Heterogeneity:** The Internet enables the users to access services and to run applications over a heterogeneous collection of computers and networks. Heterogeneity is applied on the following-

    ➢ **Computer Hardware:** For example, Mainframe, workstation, PCs services, etc.

    ➢ **Computer Software:** For example, UNIX, MS Windows, International Business Machine/ Operating System 2 (IBM OS/2) or Real-times Operating Systems, etc.

➢ **Unconventional devices:** For example, teller machines, telephone switches, robots, manufacturing systems, etc.

➢ **Diverse Networks and Protocols:** For example, Ethernet, FDDI (Fiber Distributed Data Interface), ATM (Automated Teller Machine), TCP/IP (Transmission Control Protocol/ Internet Protocol), Novell Netware, etc.

The information that all the connected computers are communicating with each other using Internet protocols is masked for different networks. Some approaches to do so are:

➢ Middleware (e.g. CORBA or Common Object Request Broker Architecture)

➢ Mobile code (e.g. Java applet)

Middleware are applied to the software layer, which provides a programming abstraction as well as masking the heterogeneity of the underlying network, hardware, operating systems and programming languages.

Mobile code is code that can be sent from one computer to the other computer and run at the destination.

2. **Openness:** The openness is the characteristic of a computer system which determines that whether the system can be extended or re-implemented in various ways. The openness of a distributed system can primarily be determined by the degree to which new resource sharing services can be added, and can be made available for use by various client programs.

The step to provide openness is to publish the interfaces of the components, but to integrate these components that are written by different programmers is a real challenge. Systems designed to support resource sharing in this way is termed as *open distributed systems*, for emphasizing the fact that they are extensible.

The open distributed systems:

➢ Can be characterized by the fact that their key interfaces are published.

➢ Are based on the provision of a uniform communication mechanism and the published interfaces for access to shared resources.

➢ Can be constructed by heterogeneous hardware and software (from different vendors, if possible). But for a system to work properly, the conformance of each component to the published standard must be tested and verified carefully.

Therefore openness cannot be achieved, if the specification and documentation of the key software of the interfaces of a system's components are made available to software developers.

3. **Security:** Security of information resources available and maintained in a distributed system is very important. Security for information resources has following components:

➢ **Confidentiality:** Protection against disclosure to unauthorized individuals.

> **Integrity:** Protection against corruption or alteration.

> **Availability:** Protection against interference with the means to access the resources.

A firewall can be used as a barrier in an intranet to protect it from outside users but it does not ensure the appropriate use of resources by users within the intranet.

To send sensitive information in a message over a network in a secure manner is a challenge. But security is not just a matter of hiding the contents of messages, it also involves knowing the identity of the user. Therefore, the second challenge is to identify the remote user. Both of the challenges can be met by using encryption techniques. Encryption is used to provide protection to shared resources and to keep sensitive information secure when it is transmitted in messages over a network. However, the two security challenges that have not yet been fully met are as follows:

> **Denial of Service Attack:** One more security problem is that a user may wish to disrupt a service for some reasons. This can be achieved by bombarding the service with a very large number of pointless requests that are not used by other users. This is called Denial-of-service (DoS) attack.

> **Security of Mobile Code:** Mobile code needs to be handled with care. Someone who receives an executable program as an e-mail attachment, the possible effects of running the programs are unpredictable.

4. **Scalability:** In a distributed system particularly in a wide area distributed system, scalability is important. According to "Neuman," a system is said to be scalable if;

"It can handle the addition of users and resources without suffering a noticeable loss of performance or increase in administrative complexity."

A system is said to be scalable if it will remain effective, when there is a significant increase in the number of users and resources. In designing a scalable distributed system, there are following challenges:

> Controlling the cost of physical resources

> Controlling the performance loss

> Preventing software resources running out

> Avoiding performance bottlenecks

5. **Failure Handling:** When there is any fault in a hardware or a software, programs may produce the incorrect results or they may halt before they have completed the intended computation.

In a distributed system, failures are partial, i.e., some components may fail while others continue its functioning. Therefore, failure handling is difficult. Following are the techniques that deal with failures:

> **Detecting Failure:** Some of the failures can be detected. For example, to

detect corrupted data in a message or a file, checksum can be used. A checksum, also known as hash sum, is a small size data computed from a random block of digital data which is used to detect errors while transmitting data.

➤ **Masking Failures:** Some of the failures that have been detected can be made less severe or hidden. For example, a file data can be written on a pair of disks so that if one gets corrupted the other one still be corrected.

➤ **Tolerating Failure:** To detect and hide all the failures in a large network is not possible. The clients of such network can be designed to tolerate failures, which generally involve the users tolerating them as well.

➤ **Recovery from Failure:** The design of software is involved in recovery. So that the state of permanent data can be "rolled back" or recovered after a server has crashed.

➤ **Redundancy:** By using redundant components, services can be made to tolerate failures. For example, in the DNS (Domain Name Server), every name table is replicated to at least two different servers.

6. **Concurrency:** In a distributed system, both the applications and the services provide resources that can be shared by clients. Therefore, there is a possibility that several clients will attempt to access the shared resource at the same time. The process that is used to manage a shared resource could take one client request at a time. But this approach limits the throughput. Therefore services and the applications usually allow multiple client requests to be processed concurrently. To keep an object safe in concurrent environment, its operations must be synchronized in such a manner that its data remains consistent. This can be achieved by a technique, such as *semaphores.*

7. **Transparency:** The aim of transparency is to make certain aspects of distribution invisible to the application programmers.

➤ **Access Transparency:** This enables the local and remote resources to be accessed using identical operations.

➤ **Location Transparency:** This enables the resources to be accessed without knowledge of their location.

➤ **Concurrency Transparency:** This enables several processes to operate concurrently using shared resources.

➤ **Replication Transparency:** This enables multiple instances of resources to be used to increase reliability and performance without having knowledge of the replicas by users or application programmers.

➤ **Failure Transparency:** It allows the users and the application programs to complete their tasks, even though they have the failure of hardware or software components.

➤ **Mobility Transparency:** The mobility of the resources and clients within a system will not affect the operation of users or programs.

➢ **Performance Transparency:** It allows the system to be reconfigured to improve performance as loads vary.

➢ **Scaling Transparency:** It allows the system and applications to expand in scale, and will not change the system structure or the application algorithms.

Test Your Progress

1. What are the goals of distributed system? List them.
2. What is transparency? Explain its types.
3. What is scalability? Why it is important for designing a distributed system?

1.5   Summary

Distributed systems are everywhere. The Internet enables the users to access its services throughout the world. Each organization manages its intranet. Small distributed system can be built from mobile computers and other small devices that can be attached to a wireless network. For constructing a distributed system resource sharing is the main motivating factor. Many challenges are there for constructing a distributed system.

1.6   Key Terms

● **CORBA:** Common Object Request Broker Architecture; provides general interface standards that can be supported by different programming languages.

● **Ethernet:** A family of computer networking technologies for local area networks.

● **FDDI:** Fiber Distributed Data Interface; a standard for data transmission in a local area network.

● **Intranets:** A computer network that uses Internet Protocol technology to share information, operational systems, or computing services within an organization.

● **Memory:** A temporary storage area.

● **NUMA:** Non-uniform Memory Access; a memory design used in multiprocessing, where the memory access time depends on the memory location relative to the processor.

1.7   Exercise

1. What are the advantages of distributed system?
2. What are the characteristics of distributed system?
3. Differentiate between the Internet and the intranet.
4. Explain various examples of distributed system.
5. What are the challenges that involve in distributed system? Explain them.
6. Discuss the issues that are relevant to the understanding of distributed, fault tolerance system, and motivation that makes it important.
7. Write the functions of semaphores.
8. Describe the types of transparency and their features.

Chapter 2
System Models

2.1   Introduction

The designing of the systems that have to be used in real world environment should be accurate. So that the systems function correctly in any circumstances and in the face of many possible difficulties and threats. Common problems faced by the designers of distributed systems are:

- **Widely and Varying Modes of Use:** The components of any system have wide variation in workload (e.g. some of the Web pages are accessed millions of times a day). Some of the applications have need for high communication bandwidth and low latency (e.g. Multimedia applications).

- **Wide Range of System Environments:** Heterogeneous hardware, operating systems, and networks must be accommodated in a distributed system (e.g. wireless networks operate at a fraction of the speed of LANs OR Local Area Networks).

- **Internal Problems:** No synchronized clock, concurrency problem, many types of software and hardware failure concerning the individual components of the system.

- **External Threats:** Attacks on data integrity, denial of service, ensuring confidentiality.

Different types of distributed systems share important underlying properties and give arise to common design problems. In this Chapter, some common properties and design issues for distributed system are given in the form of descriptive models. Each of the model provides an abstract, simple but consistent description of a relevant aspect of distributed system design.

In Section 2.2 architectural model is described, which defines the way in which the system components interacts with one another and the way in which they are mapped onto the network of computers.

In Section 2.3 fundamental models are described, which help to bring out the key problems for the designers of distributed systems. The purpose of these models is to specify the design issues, difficulties and threats which must be resolved during the development of distributed system that fulfill their task correctly, reliably and securely.

2.2   Architectural Models   [UPTU 2013]

The system architecture is its structure in terms of separately specified components and their relationship with one another. The overall aim of the system architecture is that the system will meet all the present and future demands on it. The main concern for system architecture is to make the system reliable, adaptable, manageable and cost effective.

Initially the distributed system's architectural model simplifies and abstracts the function of the individual components of a distributed system and then it considers.

● The component's placement across the network of computers, seeking to define useful pattern for the distribution of data and workload.

● The interrelationship among the components.

The initial simplification is achieved by classifying the processes as server processes, client process and peer processes. With this classification the responsibilities of each of the processes has been identified, which helps to assess their workloads and to determine the impact of failures on each of them.

For allocating work in a distributed system, there are several widely used patterns that have major impact on the performance and effectiveness of the resulting system. The actual placement of processes that built a distributed system in a network of computers is also influenced by the issues of performance, security, reliability and cost.

2.2.1 Software Layers

The term "Software architecture" refers to the structuring of software as layers or modules on a single computer and as services offered and requested among processes located on the same or different computers. The term "service layers" expresses this process and service-oriented view is shown in Figure 2.1.

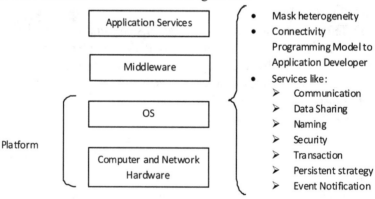

Figure 2.1: Software and Hardware Service Layers

● **Platform:**

　　➢　The lowest level hardware and software layers are referred as platform for distributed system.

> These lowest layer provide services to the upper layers.

> Enable the system's programming interface to facilitate communication and coordination among process.

> Examples are: Intel X86/windows, Intel X86/Solaris, Power PC/Mac OS X, Intel X86/Linux.

- **Middleware:**

> The purpose of middleware is to mask heterogeneity.

> It provides a convenient programming model to application programmers.

> In a set of computers (computers that interact with each other) middleware is represented by processes to implement communication and resource sharing support for distributed application.

> It provides useful building blocks for construction of software component, those who can work with each other in a distributed system.

> It also provides services that can be used by application programs.

> Examples are: CORBA (Common Object Request Broker Architecture), Java RMI (Remote Method Invocation), Microsoft's Distributed Component Object Model (DCOM), Web services, The ISO/ITU-T's (International Organization for Standardization/ International Telecommunication Union-Transmissions) Reference Model for Open Distributed Processing (RM-ODP)

> In some task application level involvement is required, which is the limitation of middleware.

2.2.2 System Architecture

The most important aspects for designing a distributed system are:

> The division of responsibilities among system components.

> The placement of components on the computers in a network.

The main architectural models on which the distribution of responsibilities is based are discussed in the following section:

- **Client/Server:** This architectural model is the most important and most widely used distributed system model. A simple structure of client/server model is shown in Figure 2.2, where client process interacts with individual server processes in a separate host computer for the purpose of accessing the shared resources that they manage.

  Servers may be clients of other servers, according to the Figure 2.2. For example, a search engine can be both a server and a client: it responds to the queries from client's browser and it runs Web crawlers that act as clients of other Web servers.

- **Peer-to-Peer:** In this type of architectural model all the processes that are involved in a task or in an activity play similar roles for interacting cooperatively as peers. There is no distinction between the client processes and the server processes.

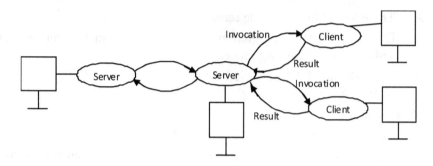

Figure 2.2: Clients invoking Individual Servers

A form of peer-to-peer application is shown in Figure 2.3. Here applications are composed up of large number of peer processes that are running on separate computer. The communication pattern among the computer depends completely on the application requirement.

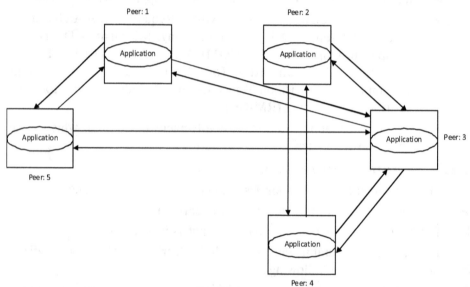

Figure 2.3: Peer-to-Peer Architecture-based Distributed Application

2.2.3 Variations in Basic Models .

By considering following aspects variation in basic models can be derived:

➢   To increase performance and resilience, multiple servers and caches can be used.

➢   Use of mobile agents and mobile codes.

➢   Low cost computers are needed by the users as they are easy to manage.

➢   Requirement to add and remove mobile devices conveniently.

●   **Services Provided by Multiple Servers:** As shown in Figure 2.4, the services that are implemented as several server processes in a separate host computer interact necessarily to provide services to the client processes. The set of objects may be partitioned by the server on the basis of services. Servers distribute these objects among themselves, or they maintain the replicated copies of those objects on several hosts.

Web provides a most common example of partitioned data, where each Web server manages its own set of resources. To increase the performance and availability and to improve fault tolerance *replication* is used.

- **Proxy servers and caches:**
  - ➤ A *cache* is a store for recently used data objects. It is closer to the client process rather than the objects themselves.
  - ➤ Whenever a new object is received by a computer, it is added up to the cache (by replacing some existing objects, if required).
  - ➤ When the client process needs an object, the caching service checks the cache for that object. If an up-to-date copy of object is available there, then it could be supplied from there to the client process.

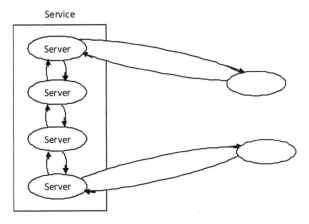

Figure 2.4: Service provided by Multiple Users

- ➤ As shown in Figure 2.5, proxy server provides a shared cache of Web resources for a client machine at a single site or across several sites.
- ➤ To increase the availability and performance of a services, by reducing the load on the WAN (Wide Area Network) and the Web servers is the main purpose of proxy servers.
- ➤ For example, it may be used for accessing remote Web servers through a firewall.
- **Mobile Code:** The most widely used and well-known example of mobile code is Applets. Whenever the user who is running a browser selects a link to an applet, (whose code is stored on the Web server), the code is downloaded to the browser and runs there.

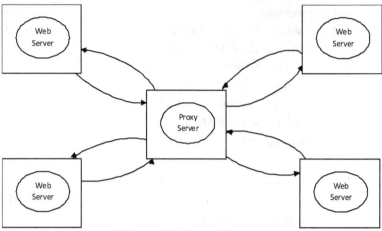

Figure 2.5: Proxy Server

The advantage of using mobile code is that it can give good interactive response as it does not suffers from the delays and/or the variability of bandwidth associated with network communication.

Security threats to the local resources in the destination computer are the main disadvantage of a mobile code.

- **Mobile Agents:**
  - ➢ It is a running program that includes both the code and the data
  - ➢ To carry out tasks on someone's behalf they travel from one computer to another in a network.
  - ➢ Invocations for local resources can be made by mobile agents at each visited site.
  - ➢ The environment that receives a mobile agent will decide that which of the local resources it should be allowed to use. This decision is based on the identity of user on whose behalf; mobile agent is acting.
  - ➢ By replacing the remote invocation with local ones to reduce communication cost and time is the advantage of mobile agents.
  - ➢ The applicability of mobile agents are limited.

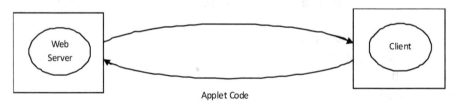

(a) Client Request Results in Downloading of Applet Code

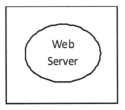 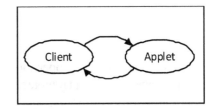

(b) Client interacts with the Applet

Figure 2.6: Web Applets

- **Network Computers:** In a desktop computer, the OS's (Operating Systems) application software require most of the active code and data to be located on a local disk. But to manage the application files and to maintain the local software base requires a high technical effort, which cannot be provided by most of the users.

  Network computer is a response for this problem. It downloads its OS and any of the application software, according to the need of user, from a remote file server. Applications run locally, but files are managed by remote file server. As all the application data and code is stored by a file server, therefore user can migrate from one network computer to another.

- **Thin Clients:** It refers to a software layer that supports a Window-based interface on a computer which is local to the user while executing programs on a remote computer. Rather than downloading the application's code into the user's computer, thin clients run them on a *compute server* (refer Figure 2.7). The *compute server* can typically be a multiprocessor or cluster computer that runs a multiprocessor version of an OS, such as UNIX or Windows NT.

  Thin client architecture is not effective in highly interactive graphical activities, such as image processing and CAD (Computer Aided Design), where the delays noticed by the users are increased according to the need to transfer image and vector information among the thin client and the application process, which results in incurring both network and OS latencies. An example of thin client is X-II Window system

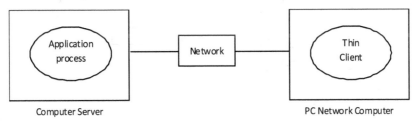

Figure 2.7: Thin Clients and Compute Server

- **Mobile Devices and Spontaneous Networking:** Now-a-days the portable devices, such as laptops, handheld devices such as PDA's (Personal Digital

Assistant), mobile phones, digital camera, wearable computer's like smart watches, and the devices that are embedded in daily appliances, such as washing machine are very popular. These portable devices provide support for mobile computing, with its proper integration into distributed system. The user take advantage of local and remote services, by carrying their mobile devices between network environments. *Spontaneous networking* describes the form of distribution that integrates mobile and other devices into a given network. The key features of spontaneous networking are as follows:

1.   Easy connection to a local network and

2.   Easy integration with local service.

Some of the limitations of spontaneous networking are as follows:

1.   Internet addressing and routing algorithms are difficult to implement.

2.   Limited connectivity.

3.   Security and privacy.

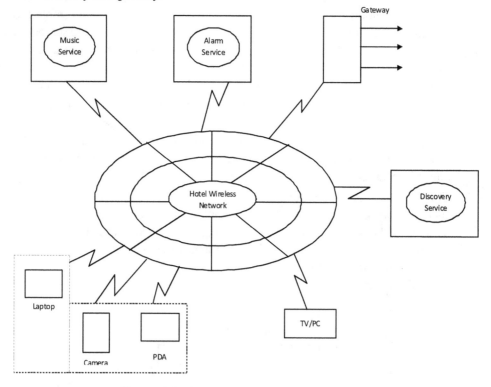

Figure 2.8: Spontaneous Network in a Hotel

- **Discovery Services:** Client processes that are running on the portable devices and on other appliances to access the services of the network to which they are connected are required by the spontaneous networking. The clients are unaware about the services that are available into the network to which these clients are connected. The purpose of discovery services is to accept and store the details of the services that are available on the network and also to respond to the queries from clients about them. The two interfaces offered by a discovery services are as follows:

1. **Registration Service:** It accepts the registration requests from the server and records the detail that they contain in the database of discovery service of currently available services.

2. **Lookup Service:** It accepts queries regarding available services and searches the database for registered service that match the queries. The result includes details that enables the client to select among several similar services based on their attributes and to make connection to one or more of them.

2.2.4 Interfaces and Objects

➢ The set of functions that are available for invocation in a server processes are specified by interface definition.

➢ In object-oriented paradigm, distributed processes can be constructed as objects, whose methods can be invoked by the remote invocation.

➢ Many of the objects can be encapsulated in server or peer processes.

➢ As per requirement of system activities, object's number type and location may change dynamically.

➢ Hence, new services can be instantiated and immediately made available for invocation.

2.2.5 Design Requirements for Distributed Architecture

Various objectives for creating a distributed system are:

➢ Sharing of computational resources

➢ Sharing of data

➢ Sharing of services

● **Performance Issues:** Performance issues of a distributed architecture are considered under the following factors:

1. **Responsiveness:** For the users of interactive application, fast and consistent response time is important. Response speed is evaluated by the load and performance of the server and the network, and the delay in all the software components that are involved. For achieving a good response time, system must be composed up of relatively few software layers and small quantities of transferred data.

2. **Throughput:** The rate at which the computational work is done for all the users in a distributed system.

3. **Load Balancing:** Without competing for the same resources it enables the applications and service processes to proceed concurrently.

● **Quality of services:** The properties that affect the Quality of services are:

1. **Reliability:** It is related to failure of fundamental model.

2.   **Performance:** The ability to meet timeliness guarantees.

3.   **Security:** It is related to security of fundamental model.

4.   **Adaptability:** The ability to meet changing resource availability and system configuration.

●   **Use of Caching and Replication:** Data replication and caching can be used by a system **to** overcome from the problems related to performance. An example is the Web-caching protocol, which is used by HTTP (HyperText Transfer Protocol) to keep caches consistent.

2.2.6 Web–caching protocol

Both the browsers and the proxy servers cache responds to client requests from the Web servers. Thus a client request may be satisfied by a response cached by either the browser or the proxy server between the client and the Web server. The cache consistency protocol is required to make sure that the browsers with fresh copies of the resource held by the Web server. This protocol works as follows:

A cached response, with the Web server cannot be validated, is used to see whether the cached copy is still up-to-date (if the cached copy is fresh). Although the Web server has knowledge of when a resource is updated, still it does not notify the browsers and proxies with caches – for the purpose of doing that the Web server would need to keep state, i.e., a record of interested browsers, proxies and HTTP (stateless protocol). To enable the browsers and the proxies to decide whether their stored responses are stale (old), Web servers respond to the request by attaching the expiry time of the resource, and the current time at the server to the response.

Browsers and proxies store the server time and expiry time together with the cached response. This enables a browser or a proxy to evaluate whether a cached response is likely to be stale (old). It is done by comparing the age of the response with the expiry time. The age of a response is the sum of the server time and the time the response has been cached. This calculation is independent of the computer clocks on the Web server and browsers or proxies agreeing with each other. If the response is stale (old), then the browser validates the cached response with the Web server. If it fails, the Web server will return a fresh response, which will be cached instead of the stale response.

●   **Dependability Issue:** Dependability is required not only in mission critical applications (e.g. command and control activities) but also in e-commerce applications where there is involvement of financial safety of the participants. Dependability of computer systems is defined as correctness, security, and fault-tolerance.

➢   **Fault Tolerance:** Continues to functioning even in the presence of failure.

➢   **Security:** Sensitive data should be located only in the secure computers.

➢   **Correctness:** Correctness of distributed concurrent programs.

Test Your Progress

1.   Explain Web–Caching protocol.

2. What are the design requirements for distributed architecture?

2.3 Fundamental Models [UPTU 2013]

The essential factors of a model are used to understand and analyze the reasons about some aspects a system's behaviour. A system model explains the following features:

- Main entities in the system.
- Method of interaction.
- Characteristics which affects their individual and collective behaviour.

  - ➤ Fundamental models provide formal description of the properties that are common in all the architectural models.
  - ➤ In these models, communication among processes is achieved by passing messages.
  - ➤ The communication over the network may get affected by delays.
  - ➤ Fundamental models can suffer by a variety of failure and also it is vulnerable to security attacks.

All the above issues are addressed by the following three models:

1. **Interaction Model:** Communication and coordination are the results of computation that occurs within processes that interact with each other by passing messages.

2. **Failure Model:** Whenever a fault occurs in any of the computers into a distributed system, it threatened the correct operation of the distributed system. This model defines and classifies the faults.

3. **Security Model:** Both external and internal agent may attack the system, because of its openness. This model defines and classifies the forms of such attack. Let us discuss each of them in brief.

2.3.1 Interaction Model [UPTU 2013]

Distributed systems are composed up of many processes who interact with each other in a very complex ways, such as:

- ➤ To provide a service, multiple server processes may cooperate with each other. For example, DNS (Domain Name server), partitions replicate data at the servers throughout the Internet.
- ➤ To achieve a common goal, a set of peer processes may cooperate with each other. For example, a voice conferencing system that distributes the stream of audio data in a similar manner but with strict real time constraints.

Distributed systems are composed up of multiple processes, the behavior and the state of these processes can be described by "distributed algorithm". This algorithm tells the steps to be taken by each process in the system, which includes the transmission of messages among the processes. Messages are transmitted among processes for the purpose of transferring information among them and to coordinate their activities.

In a distributed system, processes interact with each other by message passing, which results in communication (message passing) and coordination (synchronization and ordering of activities) among processes. Each of the process has its own state; their state can be accessed or updated by any other process. The two significant factors that affect the interacting processes in a distributed system are: (i) Communication performance is often a limiting characteristic, (ii) To maintain a global notion of time is impossible.

1. **Performance of Communication Channel:** Over a computer network, communication has following performance characteristics related to latency, bandwidth and jitter.

   ➤ The delay between the sending of a message from one process and its receipt by the other process is referred as *latency*. It includes the propagation delay, frame transmission time, and the time taken by operating system communication services at both the sending and the receiving processes, (it varies according to the current load on the operating system).

   ➤ The total amount of information that can be transmitted over a computer network in a given time is referred to as *bandwidth*.

   ➤ The variation in the time taken to deliver a series of messages is called *jitter*. It is relevant to multimedia data.

2. **Computer Clocks and Timing Events:** In a distributed system, each computer have its own internal clock, which is used by local processes to obtain the value of the current time. Therefore timestamp is associated with the events of the processes, running of different computers.

   However, if two processes read their clocks at the same time, their local clocks may supply the different time values. The reason for this is that the computer clocks drift from the perfect time and their drift rates are different from one another. The relative amount that a computer clock differs from a perfect reference clock is referred to as the *"clock drift rate"*.

   Initially if the clocks on all the computers are set to the same time, their clocks would eventually vary significantly unless some convections are applied. Several approaches are available for correcting the times on computer clocks. Clocks can be corrected by sending messages, from a computer that has an accurate time to other computers, which can still be affected by network delays. In a distributed system, setting time limits for process execution as message delivery is hard.

● **Variants of the Interaction Model:** In a distributed system it is tough to set the time limits for process execution, message delivery or clock drift. The two variants of the interaction model are:

   1. **Synchronous distributed System:** "Hadzilacos and Toug" define a synchronous distributed system in which:

      ➤ The time to execute each step of a process has known lower and upper bounds.

      ➤ Each message transmitted over a channel is received within a known bounded time.

> ➤ Each process has local clock whose drift rate from a real time has a known bound.

In a distributed system it is possible to suggest the approximate upper and lower bounds for process execution time, message delay and clock drift rates. But it is difficult to get the exact values and to provide guarantee for the chosen values. Unless the values of the bounds can be guaranteed, any design based on the chosen value will not be reliable.

2. **Asynchronous Distributed System:** An synchronous distributed system is:

> ➤ A system in which there are no bounds on:
>
> i. Process execution times
>
> ii. Message transmission delays
>
> iii. Clock drift rate
>
> ➤ A system where assumptions about the time intervals involved in any execution is not allowed.
>
> ➤ It exactly models the Internet, where browsers are designed to allow the users to do other things while they are waiting.
>
> ➤ It is more abstract and general, as a distributed algorithm that is executing on one system is likely to work also on another system.

● **Event Ordering:** In most of the cases it is required to know whether an event at one process (i.e., sending or receiving a message) has been occurred before, after, or concurrently with another event at another process. For a process in a distributed system it is impossible to have a view on the current global state of the system. The system's execution can be described in the terms of events and their order despite the lack of accurate clocks.

For example, let us consider the following set of exchanges between a group of e-mail users A, B, C and W on a mailing list:

1. User A sends a message with the subject "Hello".

2. Users B and C reply by sending a message with the subject Re: Hello;

In real time, A's message was sent first, B reads it and replies, C reads both A's message and B's reply and sends another reply with reference to both A's and B's messages. But due to the independent delays in message delivery, the messages may be delivered as shown in Figure 2.9. Some of the users may view these messages in a wrong order, such a user W might see it inbox in a following manner; if the clocks could be synchronized then:

i. Each message could carry the time of the local computer's clock when it was sent.

ii. Messages M_1, M_2 and M_3 would have times T_1, T_2 and T_3, respectively with $T_1 < T_2 < T_3$.

iii. Message received could be displayed to users according to their time order.

iv.   If the clocks are roughly synchronized then these timestamps are often in
       the correct order.

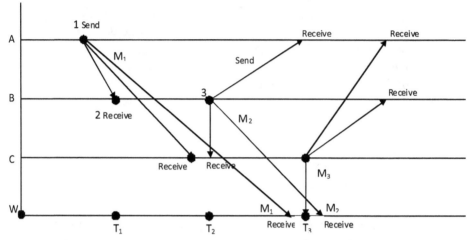

Figure 2.9: Independent Delays While Delivering Message

Since the clocks cannot be synchronized perfectly in a distributed system,
therefore a model of "Logical Time", proposed by Lamport can be used to provide
an ordering among the events at processes running at different computers in a
distributed system. The order is allowed by logical time, in which the messages are
presented to be inferred without resource to clocks. According to logical ordering,
numbers are assigned to each event (higher numbers are associated with later events).

From	Subject
C	Re: Hello
A	Hello
B	Re: Hello

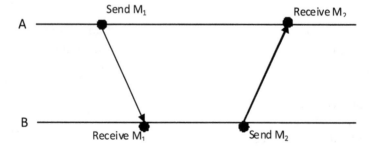

Figure 2.10

2.3.2 Failure Model

In order to provide the understanding of the effect of failures, this model defines
the ways in which failure may occur. The three types of failures are Omission failures
(process or channel failed to do something), Arbitrary failures (any type of error can

occur in processes or channels), and Timing failures (applicable only to synchronous distributed system where time limits may not be met).

- **Omission Failure:** The faults that come under the category of omission failure are, when a process or a communication channel fails to perform the actions that it is supposed to do. The two types of omission failure are as follows:

  1. **Process Omission Failure:** The main omission failure of a process is to crash, which means that the process has been halted and will not execute any further steps of its program ever. Other processes will be able to detect such crash by the fact that this process repeatedly fails to respond to invocation messages. This method of detecting crash relies on the use of "timeouts". Timeout is a method in which one process has allotted a fixed period of time for something to occur.

     A process crash can also be called fail stop, when other processes can detect certainly that the process has crashed.

  2. **Communication Omission Failures:** Let us consider the two communication primitives named 'sending' and 'receiving'. A process 'x' performs a "sending" by inserting a message 'u' in its outgoing message buffer. The communication channel transports 'u' to y's incoming message buffer. Process 'y' performs a "receiving" by taking 'u' from its incoming message buffer and then delivers it (See Figure 2.11). Operating system provides the outgoing and incoming message buffer.

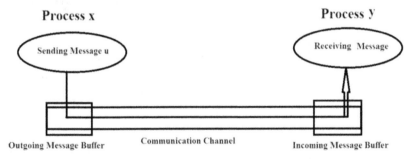

Figure 2.11: Sending and Receiving Message using Communication Channel

If a communication channel does not transport a message from x's outgoing message buffer to y's incoming message buffer, omission failure will be produced. This is known as 'dropping messages' and is caused by lack of buffer space. When a message is lost between the sending process and outgoing message buffer, it is called *sending omission failure*. When a message is lost between the incoming message buffer and the receiving process, it is called *receive omission failure*. And the loss of message in between is called *channel omission failure*.

- **Arbitrary Failures:** The worst possible failure semantics can be described by arbitrary or Byzantine failure, in which any type of error may occur. In an arbitrary failure, a process may arbitrarily omits intended processing step or it may takes unintended processing steps. Communication channel can also suffer from arbitrary failures. For example, original messages may be delivered more than once, non-existing message may be delivered, or message content may be corrupted. The omission failures are classified together with arbitrary failure as summarized in Table 2.1.

● **Timing Failure:** This type of failures are applicable in synchronous distributed systems where time limits are set for all operations. Timing is particularly relevant to computer with video and audio channels (such as multimedia computers). Video information can require a large amount of data to be transferred. For delivering such information without timing failure can make demands on the operating system and the communication system. List of timing failures are given in the Table 2.2.

Table 2.1: Classification of Failures and their Description

Class of failure	Affect	Description
Fail stop	Process	Process halts and remains halted. Other processes may detect this state.
Crash	Process	Process halts and remains halted. Other processes may not be able to detect this state.
Omission	Channel	Message inserted in an outgoing message buffer never arrives at the other end's incoming message buffer.
Send omission	Process	A process completes a send, but the message is not put in its outgoing message buffer.
Receive omission	Process	A message is put in a process's incoming message buffer, but the process does not receive it.
Arbitrary (Byzantine)	Process or channel	Process/channel exhibits arbitrary behavior. It may send/transmit arbitrary messages at arbitrary times, commit omission. A process may stop or take an incorrect step.

Table 2.2: List of Timing Failures

Class of failure	Affect	Description
Clock	Process	Process's local clock exceeds the bounds on its rate of drift from real time.
Performance	Process	Process exceeds the bounds on the interval between two steps.
Performance	Channel	A message's transmission takes longer than the stated bound.

- **Masking Failure:** In a distributed system each component is constructed from a collection of other components. Construction reliable services from the components that exhibit failures is possible. For example, multiple servers that hold the replicas of the data can continue to provide a service when one of them crashes. Having knowledge of the failure characteristic of a component can enable the new service (which is to be designed) to mask the failure of the component on which it depends. A failure can be masked by a service, either by hiding it or by converting it into a more acceptable type of failure.

- **Reliability of one-to-one Communication:** Reliable communication can be defined by the terms validity and integrity. Validity says that, the message in the outgoing message buffer is eventually delivered to the incoming message buffer. And the integrity says that, the message receive is identical to the one sent and no messages are delivered twice.

2.3.3 Security Model   [UPTU 20013]

In a distributed system security can be achieved by securing the process and channels used for their interaction and by protecting the objects that can be encapsulated against unauthorized access.

- **Protecting Objects:** Objects can be used by different users in different ways. For example, some of the objects may hold a user's private data (such as mail box) whereas others may hold shared data (such as Web). To support this, access rights are used which specify who is allowed to perform the operations of an object (that is, who is allowed to read/write?).

  Thus users are included as the beneficiaries of access rights in the model. This can be done by associating with each invocation and result the authority on which it is issued. Such an authority is called Principal (which may be a user or a process).

  It is the responsibility of a server to verify the identity of the client behind each invocation and checking their access rights on the requested objects, and the authenticity of the server can be checked by the clients.

- **Securing Processes and their Interaction:** Distributed systems are deployed and are used in tasks that are likely to be subject to external attacks by hostile users. This is true for the applications such as financial transactions, whose integrity or secrecy is crucial. Integrity can be threatened by security violations and communications failures. The threats from a potential enemy are:

  1. **Threats to Processes:** In a distributed system, a process which is designed to handle incoming requests may receive a message from any other process, and it can not necessarily determine the sender's identity. The lack of such a reliable knowledge of the source of a message is a threat to the correct functioning of both the servers and the clients. For example: spoofing.

  2. **Threats to Communication Channel:** When a message travels all across the network and its intervening gateways, an enemy can copy, alter or inject this message. Such types of attacks to the message by enemy present

a threat to the privacy and integrity of information as it travels over the network and to the system's integrity.

All these threats can be defeated by the use secure channels.

- **Secure Channels:** To build a secure channels as a service layer on top of existing communication services, encryption and authentication are used. A secure channel has following properties:
  - ➢ Each of the process reliably knows the identity of the other process.
  - ➢ Ensures the privacy and integrity of the data transmitted across it.
  - ➢ Each of the message includes a physical or logical time stamp to prevent messages from being replayed or reordered.

Test Your Progress

1. What is synchronous distributed system?
2. Explain different types of failure models.

2.4 Summary

This Chapter explained the design issues of a distributed system. Two models for distributed system have been discussed in detail. In the first section, we studied about the architectural model of a distributed system, which is concerned with the placement of its parts and the relationship between them. In the next section we described fundamental models, which are concerned with a more formal description of the properties that are common in all of the architectural model.

2.5 Key Terms

- **Buffer space:** A region of a physical memory storage used to temporarily store data while it is being moved from one place to another.
- **Client/server model:** A distributed application structure that partitions tasks or workloads between the providers of a resource or service, called servers, and service requesters, called clients.
- **Peer-to-peer:** A distributed application architecture that partitions tasks or workloads between peers.
- **Timestamp:** A temporal order among a set of events.
- **Spoofing:** A situation in which one person or program successfully masquerades as another by falsifying data and thereby gaining an illegitimate advantage.

2.6 Exercise

1. Explain various architectural models with respect to distributed system.
2. Explain various types of fundamental model.
3. Why is failure model useful in distributed system?
4. What are the various threats in the security model?
5. Define mobile code and mobile agent.
6. Explain the concept of masking failure.
7. Discuss the properties of secure channel.

Chapter 3
Theoritical Foundation

3.1   Introduction

A distributed system is a collection of independent computers that do not share a common memory. These computers communicate with each other by passing messages over a communication channel. These messages are delivered after a random time delay.

In this Chapter, firstly we will discuss the inherent limitations of a distributed systems caused by the lack of global clock and shared memory. Secondly we will discuss about how to overcome these inherent limitations.

3.2   Inherent Limitations of a Distributed System [UPTU 2007, 13, 14]

In this Section, we will discuss about the inherent limitations of a distributed system, and difficulties arise due to these limitations, such as, its impact on designing and developing a distributed system.

3.2.1 Absence of a Global Clock   [UPTU 2007, 14]

A distributed system does not have a global clock, i.e., the computers (processes) do not share a common clock. One can think that this problem can be solved either by having a common clock to all the computers or by having synchronized clocks (one at each computer). But the problem cannot be solved by any of these solutions due to the following reasons:

➤   Suppose we provide a common (global) clock for all the processes in a distributed system, In this case, due to unpredictable message transmission delays the two different processes can observe a global clock value at different instants. Therefore, these two different processes may erroneously observe two different instants in physical time to be a single instant in physical time.

➤   If each computer in a distributed system is provided their own physical clock and if we try to synchronize them, then these physical clocks can drift from the physical time and this drift rate may vary from clock-to-clock due to some technological limitations. Therefore in this case also, these two different processes may erroneously observe two different instants in physical time to be a single instant in physical time. Hence a distributed system with perfectly synchronized clocks is not possible.

3.2.2 Impact of the Absence of Global Time

Due to the absence of a global time:

➤ It is difficult in a distributed system to reason about the temporal order of events.

➤ It is difficult to design and debug algorithms for a distributed system as compared to centralized systems.

➤ Collecting up-to-date information on the state of the entire system is harder.

3.2.3 Absence of Shared Memory

As in a distributed system, computers do not share a common memory; therefore an up-to-date state of the entire system is not available to any of the individual processes. An up-to-date state of the system is required for analyzing the system's behaviour, debugging, recovering from failures, etc.

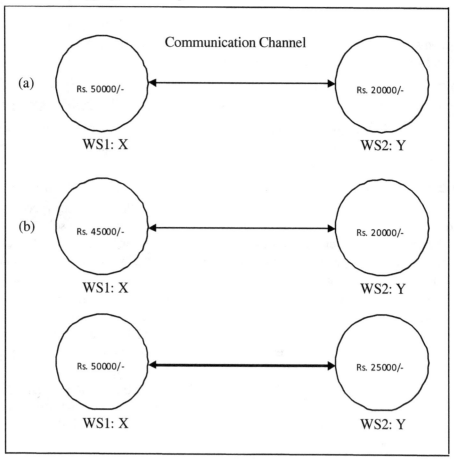

Figure 3.1: Bank Account Transactions between Two Sites in a Distributed System

In a distributed system, a process can acquire a coherent but partial view of the system or a complete but incoherent view of the system. For a system a view is said to be coherent, if all the observations of different processes are made at the same time. A complete view of a system includes the local state at all the computers and any messages that are in transit in the distributed system. A complete view is also referred to as *'global state'*. In a similar way, the global state of the distributed computation includes the local states of all the processes and any messages that are in transit between the processes. To obtain a coherent global state of the system is difficult in a distributed system, due to the absence of a global clock. Example 3.1 explains the bank account transactions between two sites WS1 and WS2.

Example 3.1: Let WS1 and WS2 are two different sites (also referred as processes in our example) of a distributed system that maintain bank accounts X and Y, respectively (refer Figure 3.1). To compute the net balance of both accounts, it may be necessary to have knowledge about the global state of the system. The initial state of both the accounts is shown in Figure 3.1(a). Let process WS1 transfers Rs. 5,000/- from account X to account Y. During the collection of global state, if site WS1 records the state of X immediately after the debit occurred, and site WS2 saves the state of Y before the fund   transfer message has received by Y, then the global system state will show Rs. 5,000/- missing as shown in Figure 3.1(b). On the other hand, if X's state is recorded before the transfer and Y's state is recorded after receiving the credit message for Rs. 5,000/, then the global system will show extra Rs. 5,000/- as shown in Figure 3.1(c). Since the state of communication channel cannot be recorded by itself. Therefore, to record the channel state, sites have to coordinate their recording activities.

The Lamport's logical clock and Vector clock are the schemes that implement an abstract virtual time to order events in a distributed system.

Test your Progress:

1.   What are the limitations of distributed system?
2.   What is meant by absence of global clock?
3.   Name the schemes that implement an abstract virtual time order events in a distributed system.

3.3   Lamport's Logical Clock [UPTU 2007, 08, 12, 13]

To order the events in a distributed system, Lamport proposed a scheme that uses the concept of logical clocks. Since a perfectly synchronized clocks and global time is absent in a distributed system, therefore on the basis of local time it is not possible to determine the order in which two events occur at two different computers. However, if it is possible to find out the order in which two events occur exclusively based on the behaviour exhibited by the underlying computation. To order the events based on the behaviour of the underlying computations, a relation is defined as follows:

3.3.1 Happened before Relationship ('!)

This relation captures the casual dependencies between the events, i.e. it tells us that whether the two events are casually related with each other or not. The definition of relation ('!) is as follows:

➢   x → y, if x and y are events in the same process and x occurred before y.

➢   x→ y, if x is the event of sending a message 's' in a process and y is the event of receiving the same message 's' by another process.

➢   If x→ y and y→ z, then x→ z, i.e., "→" relation is transitive.

Processes in a distributed system interact with each other and they can also affect the outcome of events of processes. For the purpose of designing, debugging, and understanding the sequence of execution in distributed computation, it is very important to find out the order among events. Generally an event can change the state of the system, which can influence the occurrence and outcome of the future events. That is, future events are influenced by past events and this influence between causally related events is termed as *causal affects*.

Causally Related Events

➢   An event *x* causally affects event *y* if x→y.

Concurrent Events

➢   Two distinct events x and y are said to be concurrent (x || y) if x → y and y → x, i.e., the events that do not causally affect each other are concurrent event.

➢   The relation among any two events such as x and y in a system, could be either x →y, y → x, or x || y

Example 3.2: Figure 3.2 represents a space-time diagram where a1, a2, a3, a4 are the events in process P1 and b1, b2, b3, b4 are the events in process P2 and arrow represents message transfer between the processes. For example, an arrow between a2 and b3 corresponds to a message sent from process P1 to process P2. a2 is the message sending event at P1 and b3 is the receiving event for the same message at P2.

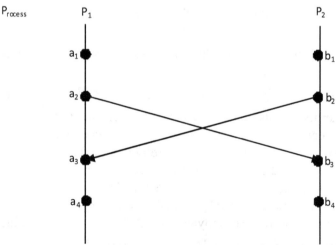

Figure 3.2: Space-Time Diagram

According to the Figure, we have b2→a3, and a3 →a4, therefore we have b2 → a4. We can also say that event b2 affects event a4. Although event a1 appears to have occurred before b1 in real time for a global observer, events b1 and a1 are concurrent.

Logical Clocks

For the purpose of understanding the relation denoted by '→', Lamport introduced the system of logical clocks. In the system each process P_i equipped with a clock C_i. Here C_i can be thought of as a function that assigns a number $C_i(x)$ to any event 'x', where $C_i(x)$ is called the timestamp of event 'x' at P_i. There is no relation with physical time, while assigning the numbers by the system of clocks. Hence it is named as *logical clocks*. The logical clocks take uniformly increasing values. For implementing these clocks, *counters* can be used.

For any events x and y:

If $x \rightarrow y$, then $C(x) < C(y)$

Now the happened before relation "!' can be realized by using the logical clocks, if the following conditions are met:

- In a process P_i for any two events 'x' and 'y', if 'x 'occurs before 'y,'

    Then $C_i(x) < C_i(y)$

- If 'x' is the event of sending a message 's' from process P_i and 'y' is the event of receiving the same message 's' at process P_j,

    Then $C_i(x) < C_j(y)$

Some **implementation rules** are available for the clocks to guarantee that the clocks satisfy the correctness conditions stated above. These **implementation rules** are as follows:

(1) Between any two successive events in process P_i, Clock C_i is incremented:

$C_i := C_i + d \ (d>0)$

If 'x' and 'y' are two successive events in P_i and x'! y, then

$C_i(y) = C_i(x) + d$

(2) If 'x' is the event of sending the message 's' by process P_i, then message 's' is assigned a timestamp $t_s = C_s(x)$. On receiving the same message 's' by process P_j, C_j is set to a value greater than or equal to its present value and greater than t_s.

$C_j := \max (C_j, t_s + d) \quad (d>0)$

In a distributed computation, the set of all the events can be totally ordered (the ordering relation is denoted by =>) using the above system of clocks as follows:

If 'x' is any event at process P_i and 'y' is any event at process P_j then x => y if and only if either

$C_i(x) < C_j(y)$ or

$C_i(x) = C_j(y)$ and $P_i < P_j$

Where ‹ is an arbitrary relation, which is used to totally order the processes to break ties. A simplest way to implement ‹ is to assign a unique identification numbers to each of the process and then $P_i < P_j$, if $i < j$.

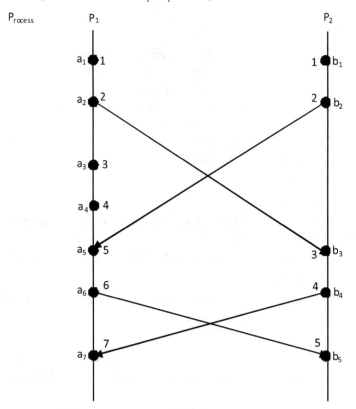

Figure 3.3: Updated Lamport's Logical Clocks

Example 3.3: Figure 3.3 shows that how Lamport's logical clocks are updated. Initially both the clock values, i.e., C1 (for process P1) and C2 (for process P2) are assumed to be 'zero' and d is assumed to be 1. In process P1, a1 is an internal event, which causes C1 to be incremented to 1 due to *implementation rule* [1]. Similarly, b1 and b2 are the events in P2 which results in C2 = 2 due to *implementation rule* [1]. a6 is a message sending event in P1 which increments C1 to 6 due to *implementation rule* [1]. Message is assigned a timestamp = 6. The event b5 (which corresponds to the receive events of the above messages), increments the clock C2 to 7 (max (4+1, 6+1)), due to both of the implementation rules. In a similar manner, b4 is a sending event in P2. Here the message is assigned a timestamp (= 4). And a7 is a receiving event of the message by event b4, at process P1. By applying both the implementation rules the clock C1 is incremented to 7 (max (6+1, 4+1)).

Virtual Time: An estimate of global/physical time is implemented through Lamport's system of logical clocks. This estimation to global/physical clock is referred to as virtual time. As virtual time gets updated along with the progression of events, hence it is discrete. If there is no event in the system, virtual time stops, whereas physical time continues its progression.

3.3.2 A Limitation of Lamports's Logical Clock [UPTU 2010]

➢   In Lamport' s system of logical clocks if $x \rightarrow y$, then

$$C(x) < C(y)$$

But if the events have been occurred in different processes, then the reverse may not be true. i.e. if 'x' and 'y' are two events in two different processes and $C(x) < C(y)$, then x '! y is not necessarily true. Hence events 'x' and 'y' may or may not be causally related.

Example 3.4: Consider Figure 3.4, which clearly shows the computation over three processes, i.e.,

$$C\ (a_1) < C\ (b_2)\ \text{and}\ C\ (a_1) < C\ (c_2)$$

From the figure it is clear that event 'a_1' is causally related to 'b_2' (as there exists a path from 'a_1' to 'b_2'), but not to 'c_2' (since no path exist from 'a_1' to 'c_2'). According to Lamport's system of logical clocks, it is assumed that the initial clock value should be 0 and value of 'd' should be 1.

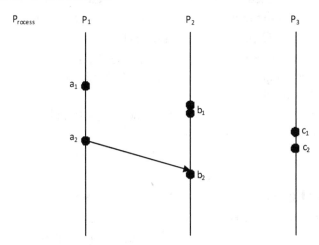

Figure 3.4: Computation over Three Processes

Therefore, in Lamport's system of logical clocks, it is true that if $C(x) > C(y)$, then y '! x, but it cannot be predicted by just looking at the timestamps of the events that events 'x' and 'y' are causally related or not.

The reason for such a limitation is that each of the clock can independently update due to the occurrence of local events in a process and the Lamport's clock system cannot differentiate among clock updates due to the local events or clock updates due to the exchange of messages between processes.

Test Your Progress

1.   What do you mean by event ordering?

2.   Explain the conditions of happens before relations.

3.   What is Lamport timestamp?

3.4   **Vector Clocks**   **[UPTU 2007, 09, 12, 13, 14]**

➢   "Fidgen" and "Mattern" independently proposed the system of vector clocks.

➢   In a distributed system, let 'n' be the number of processes. There is a clock C_i (which is an integer vector, whose length is n), at each process P_i in the system. The clock C_i can be thought of as a function that assigns a number $C_i(x)$ to any event 'x'. For an event 'x' at process P_i, $C_i(x)$ is referred to as a timestamp for that event.

➢   Corresponding to P_i's own logical time, the *i*th entry of C_i is $C_i[i]$, and the best guess of the logical time at P_j by P_i is $C_i[j]$, where $j \neq i$.

➢   For the vector clocks, the ***implementation rules*** are as follows:

(1)   In a process P_i, the clock C_i is incremented between any two successive events as:

$$C_i[i] := C_i[i] + d \qquad (d > 0)$$

(2)   If 'x' is the sending event of the message 's' by process P_i, then the message 's' is assigned a vector timestamp $t_s = C_i(x)$; C_j will be updated, after receiving the same message 's' by the process P_j, as follows:

$$\forall k, C_j[k] := \max(C_j[k], t_s[k])$$

In rule [1], sending and receiving of a message by a process is treated as events. In rule [2], a timestamp is assigned to the message after the sending process increments its clock due to rule [1].

The comparison of any two vector timestamps t^x and t^y of events x and y, respectively is as follows (compared by "Fidge"):

Equal:	$t^x = t^y$	iff	$\forall i,$	$t^x[i] = t^y[i]$;
Not Equal:	$t^x \neq t^y$	iff	$\exists i,$	$t^x[i] \neq t^y[i]$;
Less Than or Equal:	$t^x \leq d" \, t^y$	iff	$\forall i,$	$t^x[i] \, d \leq t^y[i]$;
Not Less Than or Equal To:	$t^x \nleq d" \, t^y$	iff	$\exists i,$	$t^x[i] > t^y[i]$;
Less Than:	$t^x < t^y$	iff	$(t^x \leq d" \, t^y$	$\wedge \; t^x \neq t^y)$;
Not Less Than:	$t^x \nleq t^y$	iff	$\neg (t^x \leq d" \, t^y$	$\wedge \, t^x \neq t^y)$;
Concurrent:	$t^x \parallel t^y$	iff	$(t^x \nleq t^y$	$\wedge \, t^y \nleq t^x)$;

The relation "$\leq$" is a partial order.

3.4.1 **Causally Related Events**

Two events 'x' and 'y' are said to be causally related, if $t^x < t^y$ or $t^y < t^x$. If the events are not causally related, then these events are concurrent. In a vector clock's system:

$$x' \rightarrow y \qquad \text{iff} \qquad t^x < t^y$$

Therefore, vector's clock system allows the user to order the events and to decide whether two events are causally related or not simply by observing the timestamp of the events. This is not possible in Lamport clock, because $t^x \rightarrow t^y$, does not always implies that x → y.

Example 3.5 As an example consider Figure 3.5, which illustrates that how clocks are updated and how time is distributed in the system using vector clocks. Initially the clock values are zero and 'd' is assumed to be 1. Distribution of time in vector clocks for Figure 3.5 is as follows:

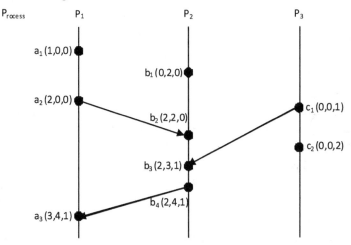

Figure 3.5: Distribution of Time in Vector Clock

- For P1, a1 is an internal event that causes $C_1[1] = 1$ (due to *implementation rule* [1]).
- For P1, a2 is a message sending event which causes $C_1[1] = 2$ (due to *implementation rule* [1]).
- For P2, b2 is message receiving event which causes $C_2[2] = 2$ (due to *implementation rule* [1]).
- And $C_2[1] = 2$ (due to *implementation rule* [2]).
- For P3, c1 is a message sending event which causes $C_3[3] = 1$ (due to *implementation rule* [1]).
- For P2, b3 is a message receiving event which causes $C_2[2] = 3$ (due to *implementation rule* [1]).
- And $C_2[3] = 1$ (due to *implementation rule* [2]).
- For P2, b4 is a message sending event which causes $C_2[2] = 4$ (due to *implementation rule* [1]).
- For P1, a3 is a message receiving event which causes $C_1[1] = 3$ (due to *implementation rule* [1]).
- And $C_1[2] = 4$ and $C_1[3] = 1$ (due to *implementation rule* [2]).

Test Your Progress

1. Who proposed the system of vector clocks?
2. What are vector clocks? What are its advantages over Lamport clock?

3.   What are the problems with Lamport clock, which are solved by vector clock?

3.5 Causal Ordering of Messages
[UPTU 2007, 08, 09, 12]

"Birman and *Joseph"* was the first who proposed the causal ordering of messages. The idea behind the causal ordering of messages is to maintain the same causal relationship that holds among the events of "message sending" and their corresponding "message receiving" events. Causal ordering of messages are different from causal ordering of events (it deals with the idea of causal relationship among events).

Techniques for causal ordering of messages play a vital role for the purpose of developing the distributed algorithms and to simplify those algorithms. If causal ordering of messages is not present, then it is compulsory to check each and every update to make sure that it does not violate the consistency constraints.

For the causal ordering of messages in the distributed system, there are two protocols that use vector clocks. The first protocol is *Birman-Schiper-Stephenson Protocol*, which was implemented in ISIS (Intermediate System to Intermediate System). In this protocol, processes are assumed to communicate only through broadcast messages. The second protocol is *Schiper-EGGLI-Sandoz Protocol*, which does not require processes to communicate only through broadcast messages. The requirement for both the protocols is that the messages should be delivered reliably, i.e., lossless and uncorrupted messages should be delivered.

Basic Idea: For both the protocols, the basic idea is that the message will be delivered to the process only if the process has been received a message which was immediately preceding it. Otherwise, the message will not be delivered immediately to the process but it will be buffered until the message which was immediately preceding it is delivered. A vector associated with each message contains the necessary information for a process to decide whether there exists a message preceding it or not.

Birman-Schiper-Stephenson Protocol

1.   A process P_i increments the vector time V_{Pi} [i] and timestamps 's' before broadcasting a message 's'.

2.   Upon receiving message 's', a process $P_j \neq P_i$, timestamped V_s from P_i and delays its delivery until both the following conditions are satisfied:

   (a) V_{Pj} [i] = V_s [i] – 1

   (b) V_{Pj} [k] ≥ V_s [k] $\forall$ k $\in$ {1, 2 , . . . , n} - {i}
   (Here 'n' is the total number of processes.)

   At each process delayed messages are queued in a queue, which is sorted by vector time of the message. The order of concurrent messages are provided by the time of their receipt.

3. V_{Pj} is updated when a message is received at a process P_j, according to the

vector clocks implementation rule [2].

Step 2(a) states that all the messages from Process P_i that precede 's', has been received by process P_j and Step 2(b) states that P_j has received all those messages received by P_i before sending 's'.

Schiper-EGGLI-Sandoz Protocol
Data Structures and Notations

Each of the process P maintains a vector which is denoted by V_P and whose size is (n-1), where 'n' is the total number of processes in the system. An element of V_P is an ordered pair (P', t) where P' is the identity (ID) of the destination process of a message and t is a vector timestamp. It is assumed that vector clocks are used by the processes in the system. Following are the notations used for describing the protocol:

- t_S = logical time at the sending of message S.
- t_{Pi} = present/ current logical time at process P_i.

The Protocol

- **Sending of a Message S from Process P1 to Process P2**
- Send a timestamped message 'S' to process P_2 along with V_P_1.
- Then insert pair (P_2, t_S) into V_P_1. If V_P_1 already contains a pair (P_2, t), it simply gets overwritten by the new pair (P_2, t_S). The pair (P_2, t_S) was not sent to P_2. In future any message carrying the pair (P_2, t_S) cannot be delivered to P_2 until $t_S < t_{P2}$.
- **Arrival of a Message S at Process P2**

  If V_S (the vector associated with message S) does not contain any pair (P_2, t)

  > Then the message can be delivered

  > > Else

  > > > If $t < t_{P2}$ then

  > > > The message cannot be delivered (* it will be buffered for later delivery *)

  > > Else

  > > > The message can be delivered.

If message S can be delivered at process P_2, then the following actions are taken:

1. Merge V_S (accompanying S) with V_P_2 in the following manner :
   - If ($\exists$(P, t) $\in$ V_S, such that P $\neq$ P_2) and ($\forall$ (P', t) $\in$ V_P_2, P' $\neq$ P), then (P, t) will be inserted into V_P_2. This rule performs the following:

     If in V_P_2 there is no entry for process P and V_S contains an entry for process P, then insert that entry into V_P_2.
   - $\forall$ P, P $\neq$ P_2, if ((P, t) $\in$ V_M) $\wedge$ ((P, t') $\in$ V_P_2), then the following actions will be taken by the algorithm:

The pair $(P, t) \in V\_P_2$ can be substituted by the pair (P, t_{sub}) where t_{sub} is such that $\forall$ i, t_{sub} [i] = max (t [i], t' [i]).

The algorithm satisfies the following two conditions, due to the above two actions:

i.   No message can be delivered to P until t' $< t_p$ is not true.

ii.   No message can be delivered to P until t $< t_p$ is not true.

2.   Update the logical clock of site P_2.

3.   Since local clock has been updated, therefore check the buffered messages that can now be delivered.

After ensuring that the pair (P, t) is no longer needed, it can be deleted from the vector maintained at a site.

Test Your Progress

1.   What is causal ordering of messages?

2.   Explain total ordering of messages?

3.   Describe Schiper–EGGLI–Sandoz algorithm.

4.   Describe Birman–Schiper–Stephenson algorithm.

3.6   Global State   [UPTU 2009, 10]

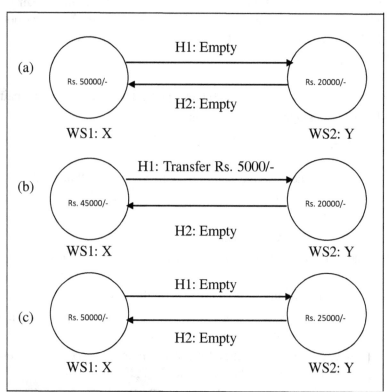

Figure 3.6: Global States and their Transitions in Bank Account

In a distributed system collecting or recording a consistent (coherent) global state is a challenging task and this is because of the lack of global clock and shared memory.

Figure 3.6 represents the global states and their transitions in the bank account example (See Example 3.1). The Figure shows the stages of a computation when Rs. 5000/- is transferred from account 'X' to account 'Y'. Figure 3.6(a) represents the Global state 1, Figure 3.6(b) represents the Global state 2, and Figure 3.6(c) represents the Global state 3.

A global state may be inconsistent if $n < n'$, where 'n' is the total number of messages sent by 'X' along with the channel before X's state was recorded and 'n''' is the total number of messages sent by 'X' along with the channel before channel's state was recorded. A global state may also be inconsistent if $n > n'$. Hence for a consistent global state following conditions are required:

$$n = n'$$

or

$$m = m'$$

Where 'm' is the total number of messages received along with the channel before Y's state was recorded and 'm''' is the total number of messages received along with the channel by 'Y' before channel's state was recorded.

Since there is no such system available in which the number of messages sent along with the channel is less than the number of messages received along the channel. That is:

$$n' \geq m$$

Therefore

$$n \geq m$$

In other words, "in a consistent global state, the state of a communication channel should be the sequence of messages sent along with the communication channel before the sender's state was recorded, excluding the sequence of messages received along with the channel before the receiver's state was recorded".

Definitions

Local States: The local state of a computer (site) WS_i, at a given time is defined by the local context of the distributed application. Let LWS_i denote the local state of WS_i at any time.

Let   send (s_{ij}); the send event of message s_{ij} by WS_i to WS_j .

Rec (s_{ij}); the receive event of message s_{ij} by site WS_j .

Time (w); the time at which state w was recorded.

Time (send (s)); the time at which event send (s) occurred.

For a message s_{ij} sent by WS_i to WS_j, we say that:

- send $(s_{ij}) \in LWS_i$ iff time (send (s_{ij})) < time (LWS_i).
- rec $(s_{ij}) \in LWS_j$ iff time (rec(s_{ij})) < time (LWS_j).

For the local states LWS_i and LWS_j of any two computers (sites) WS_i and WS_j, two sets of messages are defined as follows:

- **transit (LWS_i, LWS_j)** =$\{s_{ij} \mid$ send $(s_{ij}) \in LWS_i \wedge$ rec$(s_{ij}) \in LWS_j\}$
- **inconsistent (LWS_i, LWS_j)** = $\{s_{ij} \mid$ send (s_{ij}) " LWS_i '" rec(s_{ij}) " $LWS_j\}$

Global State: A global state (G) of a system is a collection of all the local states of its sites. That is. G = $\{LWS_1, LWS_2,....LWS_n\}$, where 'n' is the total number of computers (sites) in the system.

Consistent Global State: A global state G = $\{LWS_1, LWS_2,....LWS_n\}$ is consistent iff:

$$\forall i, \ \forall j: 1 \leq i, j \leq n :: \text{inconsistent } (LWS_i, LWS_j) = \phi$$

Transitless Global State: A global state is transitless iff:

$$\forall i, \ \forall j: 1 \leq i, j \leq n :: \text{transit } (LWS_i, LWS_j) = \phi$$

Strongly Consistent Global State

A global state is said to be strongly consistent if it is consistent and transitless. That is, in this not only the sending events of all the recorded received events are recorded, but also the receive events of all the recorded sending events are recorded.

Example 3.6: The global state (G) for the set of local states shown in Figure 3.7 is:

G = $\{LWS_{11}, LWS_{21}, LWS_{31}\}$, which is strongly consistent because:

$\forall i, \ \forall j, 1 \leq I, j < 3$

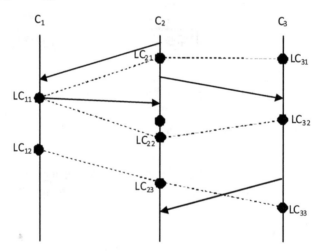

Figure 3.7: Global State in Distributed Computation

3.6.1 Chandy-Lamport's Global State Recording Algorithm [UPTU 2012]

Lamport and Chandy were the first who proposed a distributed algorithm for capturing a consistent global state. The algorithm uses a special message "Marker" to initiate the algorithm. This marker has no effect on the underlying computation. The communication channels are anticipated to be "First In First Out" (FIFO). The recorded global state can also be referred as a *snapshot* of the system state.

Marker Sending Rule for a Process P:

- P records its state.
- For each outgoing channel 'H' from process 'P' on which a marker has not been already sent, P sends a marker along H before P sends further messages along H.

Marker Receiving Rule for a Process Q:

On receiving a marker along with the channel 'H':

    If Q has not recorded its state

        Then

            Begin

                Record the state of H as an empty sequence.

                Follow the "Marker Sending Rule."

            End

        else

Record the state of H as the sequence of messages received along H after Q' s state was recorded and before Q received the marker along C.

The global state recording algorithm can be initiated by any of the process just by executing the "Marker Sending Rule". Several processes can also initiate this algorithm concurrently, with each process getting its own version of a consistent global state. A simple way for collecting all the recorded information for each process is to send the information it recorded to the initiator of the recording process.

The recorded global state is useful because it is able to detect stable properties such as the termination of a communication and a deadlock among processes. If a stable property holds before the execution of recording algorithm begins, then it continues to hold, and will therefore be included in the recorded global state.

Test Your Progress

1.   Explain the concept of global state.

3.7   Termination Detection   [UPTU 2014]

In a distributed computation, it is important to have knowledge about when the computation has terminated. In many distributed algorithms and computations, the problem of termination detection arises. For example; how to determine when a deadlock detection, an election, a token generating algorithm, or a deadlock resolution has terminated. Basically Termination Detection, is an example of the usage of the coherent view (consistent global state) of a distributed system. The termination detection algorithm was proposed by "Huang".

System Model: A process can either be in active state or in idle state. A process in an idle state can become active after receiving the *computation message*. The messages that are related to the underlying computation being performed by the cooperating processes are *"computation message"*. The situation when all the processes are idle and there are no messages in transit, we say that the computation has terminated. The messages that are sent by the termination detection algorithm are referred to as *"control messages"*.

Basic Idea: One of the cooperating processes monitors the computation. This cooperating process is called the "controlling agent". Initially all the processes are idle, the weight of the controlling agent is 1, and the weight of the rest of the processes is 0. The moment when the controlling agent sends a computation message to one of the processes, computation starts. Whenever a process sends a message, the process's weight is split between the sending process and the receiving process. The weight that has been received along with a message is added to the weight of the process. Therefore in the algorithm a weight W $(0 \leq W \leq 1)$ is assigned to each active process and to each message in transit. Weight assigned should satisfy the following invariant:

At any time, $\Sigma W = 1$;

When the computation is finished, a process sends its weight to the controlling agent, this agent adds the received weight to its own weight. When the weight of the controlling agent is once again becomes equal to 1, it concludes that the computation has terminated.

Notations: In the algorithm following notations are used:

- B (DW) = Computation message sent as a part of the computation and DW is the weight assigned to it.

- C (DW) = Control message sent from the processes to the controlling agent and DW is the weight assigned to it.

Huang's Termination Detection Algorithm

Rule 1. The controlling agent or an active process having weight W may send a computation message to process P by doing:

Drive W_1 and W_2 such that

$W_1 + W_2 = W, W_1 > 0, W_2 > 0$;

$W := W_1$;

Send B (W_2) to P;

Rule 2. On receiving B (DW), a process P having weight W does:

$W := W + DW$;

If P is idle, P becomes active;

Rule 3. An active process having weight W may become idle at any time by doing:

Send C (W) to the controlling agent;

W := 0;

(The process becomes idle);

Rule 4. On receiving C (DW), the controlling agent having weight W takes the following actions:

W := W + DW;

If W = 1, concludes that the computation has terminated.

Test Your Progress

1. What is termination detection problem?

2. Define Process.

3. Explain Huangs algorithm.

3.8   Summary

The main concentration area for this Chapter is the two characteristics of a distributed system. i.e., absence of global clock and absence of shared memory. This Chapter explained about the Lamport's logical clocks and vectors clocks for ordering the events in a distributed system and their importance in designing distributed algorithms. In the next Section, we addressed the problem of recording global states in the absence of global clock and shared memory. We then described Chandy–Lamport's algorithm that can collect a consistent global state. Finally the last section explained the problem of termination detection.

3.9   Key Terms

- **Counters:** A device which stores the number of times a particular event or process has occurred in terms of a clock signal.

- **Protocol:** A set of rules or procedures for transmitting data between electronic devices, such as computers.

- **Vector clock:** An algorithm which generates a partial ordering of events in a distributed system and detecting causality violations.

- **Virtual time:** A new concept for organizing and synchronizing distributed systems which can be applied to distributed database concurrency control.

3.10   Exercise

1. What could be the impact of absence of global clock and shared memory? Explain with the help of suitable example.

2. What are Lamport's logical clock?

3. For a Lamport clock system, prove that for any two events 'a' and 'b' if a→b, then C(a) < C(b), but vice versa is not true.

4. Why does a logical clock need to be implemented in distributed system?

5. What do you mean by consistent global state?

Practice with Ease for Examination

1. What are distributed systems? Name two advantages and disadvantages of distributed system over centralized ones. State in your own words the concept of parallelism transparency.   [2006 - 07]

    Ans: See Section 1.1

    Advantages: Reliability and Incremental Growth

    Disadvantages: Security and Network

    Parallelism transparency permits parallel activities without users knowing how, where, and when these activities are carried out.

2. Give five types of hardware resources and five types of software resources that can be shared. Give example of their sharing as it occurs in distributed system.   [2006 - 07]

    Ans: See Section 1.3

3. What are distributed system? Explain its challenges in brief.   [2007 - 08]

    Ans: See Sections 1.1 and 1.4

4. What are distributed systems? What are significant advantages and limitations of distributed system? Explain with the example, what could be the impact of absence global clock and shared memory?   [2008 - 09]

    Ans: See Section 1.1 and 3.2. Also see Example 3.1

5. Why is scalability an important feature in the design of distributed system? Discuss some of the guiding principles for designing a scalable distributed system.   [2008 - 09]

    Ans: See Section 1.4

6. How the resource sharing done in distributed system? Explain with example.   [2009 - 10]

    Ans: See Section 1.3

7. Discuss the Web challenges for implementing distributed system. [2009 - 10]

    Ans: See Section 1.3

8. Discuss the limitations of distributed system.   [2009 - 10]

    Ans: See Section 1.1

9. How the distributed computing system is better than the parallel processing system? Explain.   [2013 - 14]

    Ans: See Section 1.1.4

10. Define the term transparency. Explain important types of transparencies in distributed system.   [2013 - 14]

    Ans: See Section 1.4

11. Discuss the major issue in designing a distributed system.   [2012 - 13]

    Ans: See Section 1.4

(Transparency, communication, performance and scalability, heterogeneity, openness, reliability and fault tolerance, security)

12. Discuss the various advantages and disadvantages of the various commonly used models for configuring distributed computing systems.   [2012 - 13]

    [Hint: Advantages and disadvantages of centralized system and parallel system over distributed computing system.]

13. What is distributed system? What are the various threats of distributed system?
                                                                    [MTU 2012 - 13]

    Ans: See Section 1.1.

    Threats of distributed system:

    ● Eavesdropping (obtaining copies of messages without authority).

    ● Masquerading (sending/receiving the message using others identity).

    ● Message tampering (altering message content on its way in a store and forward net).

    ● Replaying (storing message and sending them at later time).

14. What is process? Explain the various states of process using state transition diagram.   [MTU 2012 - 13]

    Ans: In computing, a process is an instance of a computer program that is being executed. It contains the program code and its current activity.

    Process States: New, Ready, Running, Waiting, and Terminated

15. Why is computer clock synchronization necessary? Describe the design requirement for a system to synchronize the clock in a distributed system.
                                                                    [2006 - 07]

    Ans: Major design requirement for a system to synchronize the clock in a distributed system are:

    (i)   There should be a limit on deviation between clocks or between any clock and UTC (Coordinated Universal Time).

    (ii) Clocks should only ever advance.

    (iii) Only authorized principals may reset clock.

    Practically (i) cannot be achieved unless only benevolent failures are assumed to occur and the system is synchronous.

16. What are vector clocks? What are the advantages of vector clocks over Lamport clock?   [2006 - 07]

    Ans: See Section 3.4

17. Construct a solution to reliable, totally ordered multicast in a synchronous system, using a reliable multicast and a solution to the consensus problem.
                                                                    [2006 - 07]

    Ans: See Section 3.5

18. What are the logical clocks? Why does a logical clock need to be implemented

in distributed system? Explain with an example, what are the impacts of absence of global clock and shared memory?   [2007 - 08]

Ans: See Sections 3.2 and 3.3

19. What do you mean by causal ordering of messages? Discuss the salient features of broadcast based protocols that make the use of vector clock which ensures causal ordering of messages.   [2007 - 08]

Ans: See Section 3.5 and see Birman-Schiper-Stephenson Protocol

20. What do you mean by global state of the distributed system? What are the differences between consistent global state, Transitless global state and strongly consistent state?   [2008 - 09]

Ans: See Section 3.6

21. What are the vector clocks? Explain with the help of implementation rule of vector clocks, how they are implemented? What are the advantages of vector clock over Lamport clock? For the space-time diagram shown below, obtain the vector timestamp of various events.   [2008 - 09]

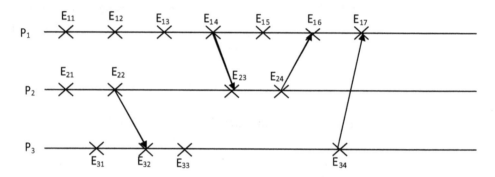

Figure 3.8

Ans: See Section 3.4

22. What do you mean by causal ordering of message? If process P sends two messages M1 and M2 to another process Q, what problem may arise if the two messages are not received by recipient Q, in the order they were sent by process P. Develop an algorithm which guarantees the causal ordering of message in distributed system.   [2008 - 09]

Ans: See Section 3.5

Explanation: Schiper-EGGLI-Sandoz Protocol

23. What do you mean by global state of distributed system? Also explain the main features of consistent global state.   [2009 - 10]

Ans: See Section 3.6

24. Discuss the limitation of Lamport's logical clock with suitable example.

                                                         [2011 - 12]

Ans: See Section 3.3.1

25. Give the Chandy–Lamport's global state recording algorithm.　　[2011 - 12]

    Ans: See Section 3.6.1

26. Discuss vector clock. Explain the implementation rules for vector clocks. Give the vector timestamp of messages for the following examples, where s1, s2 and s3 represent sites.　　[2011 - 12]

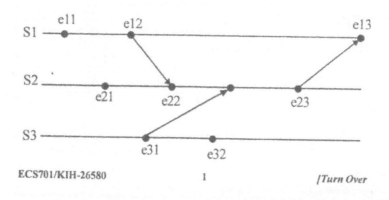

ECS701/KIH-26580　　　　　　　1　　　　　　　*[Turn Over*

Figure 3.9

Ans: See Section 3.5

27. Discuss the causal ordering of messages. Give any algorithm which can order the messages according to causal dependencies.　　[2011 - 12]

    Ans: See Section 3.5

28. How Lamport clock causally relates two events? Discuss the limitation of Lamport clock. How the vector clock remove the limitation of Lamport clock? Explain.　　[2012 - 13]

    Ans: See Sections 3.3 and 3.4

29. What is logical clock? What are the limitations of Lamport clock?

    [MTU 2012 - 13]

    Ans: See Section 3.3

30. Write short notes on the following:

    i.　Total causal order

    ii.　Synchronous Vs asynchronous computing　　[MTU 2012 - 13]

    Explanation:

    Total causal order: If a correct process delivers message P1 before P2, then any other correct process that delivers P2 will have already delivered P1.

    Synchronous Vs asynchronous computing:

    In asynchronous computing,

    1.　No processors are synchronized, and there is no bound on drift rate of clocks.

2.   Message delays are ûnite but unbounded.

3.   There is no bound on time to execute a step at a process.

Synchronous computing:

1.   Processors are synchronized and clock drift rate is bounded.

2.   Message delivery occurs in one logical step.

3.   Upper bound is known on time to execute a step at a process.

31. Discuss the impact of the absence global clock in a distributed system.

[2013 - 14]

Ans: See Section 3.2

32. What is termination detection in distributed system? Explain any algorithm for termination detection.   [2013 - 14]

Ans: See Section 3.7

33. What is vector clock? How does it maintain causal ordering? Explain.

[2013 - 14]

Ans: See Section 3.3

Unit-II

Distributed Mutual Exclusion: Classification of distributed mutual exclusion, requirement of mutual exclusion theorem, Token-based and Non-token based algorithms, performance metric for distributed mutual exclusion algorithms.

Distributed Deadlock Detection: system model, resource Vs communication deadlock prevention, avoidance, detection & resolution, centralized dead lock detection, distributed deadlock detection, path pushing algorithms, edge chasing algorithms.

Chapter 4
Distributed Mutual Exclusion

4.1   Introduction

The goal is the sharing of some critical resource between processes using only one process at a time-this is the problem generally occurred in time-sharing systems.

The solution is to allow access in a specially-marked block of code called a critical section in such a way that and only one process can be in a critical section at a particular instant of time T.

A mutual exclusion protocol takes guarantee of it in an asynchronous shared-memory model.

The processes are cycled between states trying (try to get in the critical section), critical (in critical section), exiting (to allow other processes to enter their critical sections), and remainder (everything else). The process decides only in the trying and exiting states when to switch to the next state by running the mutual exclusion protocol; it switches to the next state by its own in the critical or remainder states.

4.2   Classification of Distributed Mutual Exclusion

Generally we are using two types of mutual exclusion protocol.

- **Non-Token based:** There are two or more successive rounds of messages exchange takes place among the sites to determine the site which will enter the CS next.

- **Token-based:** A unique token (known as privilege message) passes around from one site to another. Following are the features of token-based mutual exclusion protocol:

➢   All sites share a unique token.
➢   Only that site which possesses the token can enter its CS.
➢   Mutual exclusion is ensured because of the uniqueness of the token.

Test Your Progress

1.   What is meant by critical section?
2.   Explain classification of mutual exclusion.
3.   State the features of token-based mutual exclusion protocol.

4.3   Preliminaries

Required System Model

The system consists of N sites, WS1, WS2, ..., WSTN. We assume that a single process runs on each site. Pi denotes the process running at site WSi. There can be the following three states of a site: requesting to enter the CS, executing in the CS and neither requesting nor executing the CS (i.e., idle). In the 'requesting the CS' state, the site is blocked and is not allowed to make more requests for the CS. In the 'idle' state, the site is executing outside the CS. In token-based algorithms, there can be a state when a site holding the token executes outside the CS (called the *idle token state*). At any instant, several pending requests for CS may exist for a site. A site queues up all these requests and serves them one at a time.

4.3.1 Requirement of Mutual Exclusion

Following factors decide the requirement of mutual exclusion:

●   **Safety Property:** At any instant of time T, a single process can be in the critical section.

●   **Liveness Property:** This property ensures that the sites will be deadlock and starvation free. Two or more sites should wait for messages but for a limited period of time.

●   **Fairness:** Fairness property ensures that the CS execution requests will be executed according to the order of their arrival time (calculated by a logical clock-c) in the system.

4.3.2 Performance Metric for Distributed Mutual Exclusion

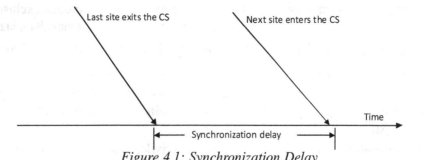

Figure 4.1: Synchronization Delay

Releasing the Critical Section

- Site WS_i, after exiting from the CS, removes its request from the request queue top and broadcasts a time stamped RELEASE message to all other sites.

- When a site WS_j receives a RELEASE message from site WS_i, it removes WS_i's request from its request queue.

On removing a request from its request queue, a site own request may come at the top of the queue, which enables it to enter the CS.

Theorem: Lamport's algorithm achieves mutual exclusion

Proof:

Proof is by contradiction. Suppose two sites WS_i and WS_j are executing the CS concurrently. For this to be happen conditions L1 and L2 must hold concurrently at both the sites.

This implies that at some instant of time T, say t, both WS_i and WS_j requests are at the top of their request queues and condition L1 holds them. Without loss of generality, assume that WS_i's request has smaller value of timestamp than the request of WS_j.

At instant t it is clear that from L1 and FIFO property of the communication channel that WSi request must be present in request-queue$_j$ when WSj was executing its CS. This implies that WS_j's request is at the top of its own request queue when a smaller timestamp request, WS_i's request, is present in the request-queue$_j$ – a contradiction!

Theorem: Lamport's algorithm is fair

Proof:

The proof is by contradiction. Suppose a site WS_i's request timestamp value is smaller than the request of another site WS_j and WS_j is able to execute the CS before WS_i.

To execute in the CS, WS_j has to satisfy the conditions L1 and L2. This implies that at some instant of time say t, WS_j own request should be at the top of its queue and it has also received a message with lager timestamp value than the timestamp of its request from all other sites.

But request queues are ordered by timestamp, and we assume that WS_i has lower timestamp, so WS_i's request must be placed ahead of the WS_j's request in the request-queue$_j$. This is a contradiction!

Performance

For each CS execution, Lamport's algorithm requires (N – 1) REQUEST messages, (N – 1) REPLY messages, and (N – 1) RELEASE messages. Thus, in a total, Lamport's algorithm requires 3(N – 1) messages per CS execution. T is the Synchronization delay of the algorithm.

An Optimization

In Lamport's algorithm, omitting of REPLY messages can exist in certain situations. For example, if site WS_j receives a REQUEST message from site WSi after it has sent its own REQUEST message with timestamp higher than the timestamp of site WS_i's request, then site WSj need not send a REPLY message to site WS_i .

This is because when site WS_i receives site WS_j's request with timestamp higher than its own, it concludes that site WS_j does not have any pending smaller timestamp request.

With this optimization, Lamport's algorithm requires between $3(N - 1)$ and $2(N - 1)$ messages per CS execution.

4.5.2 Ricart-Agrawala Algorithm

The Ricart-Agrawala algorithm uses the FIFO property for communication channels. It uses two types of messages namely REQUEST and REPLY. In order to enter the critical section, a process sends a REQUEST message to all other processes. For giving permission to that process, it sends a REPLY message to the process. Lamport-style logical clocks are used to assign a timestamp to critical section requests which are further used to calculate the priority of requests priority. Each process pi maintains the Request-Deferred array, RD_i , whose size is equal to the number of processes in the system. Initially, $\forall i \ \forall j : RD_i [j] = 0$. Whenever pi defers the request sent by pj, it sets $RD_i [j] = 1$ and after it has sent a REPLY message to pj, it sets $RD_i [j] = 0$.

Algorithm

Requesting the Critical Section

(a)   In order to enter the CS, site WSi broadcasts a time-stamped REQUEST message to all other sites.

(b)   After receiving a REQUEST message from site WSi, site WSj sends a REPLY message to site WSi if site WSj is neither requesting nor executing the CS, or if the site WSj is requesting and WSi's request's timestamp is smaller than site WSj's own request's timestamp.

Otherwise, the reply is deferred and WSj sets $RD_j [i] = 1$.

Executing the Critical Section:

(c)   After receiving a REPLY message from every site to which it sent a REQUEST message, Site WSi enters the CS.

Releasing the Critical Section

(d)   After exiting from the CS, site WSi sends all the deferred REPLY messages: "j if RDi [j] = 1, then send a REPLY message to WSj and set $RD_i [j] = 0$.

Notes: After receiving a message, site WSi updates its clock-c using the timestamp. After taking the request for the CS for processing, a site updates its local clock and assigns a timestamp to the request.

Correctness

Theorem: Ricart-Agrawala algorithm achieves mutual exclusion.

Proof:

Proof is by contradiction. Suppose two sites WSi and WSj are concurrently executing in the CS and WSi's request has higher priority than the request of WSj. Clearly, WSi receives WSj's request after it makes its own request. Thus, WSj and WSi can concurrently execute the CS if WSi returns a REPLY to WSj (in response to WSj's request) before the exit of WSi from the CS. However, this is impossible as WSj's request has lower priority. Therefore, Ricart-Agrawala algorithm achieves mutual exclusion.

Performance

Ricart-Agrawala algorithm requires $(N - 1)$ REQUEST messages and $(N - 1)$ REPLY messages, for each CS execution. Thus, it requires $2(N - 1)$ messages per CS execution. Synchronization delay in the algorithm is T.

4.5.3 Maekawa's Algorithm

Maekawa's algorithm was the first mutual exclusion algorithm based on quorum. The request sets for sites (i.e., quorums) are made in order to satisfy the following conditions:

M1: ($\forall$ i $\forall$ j : i 6 = j, $1 \leq$ i, j $\leq$ N :: Ri$\cap$ Rj 6 = -)

M2: ($\forall$ i : $1 \leq$ i $\leq$ N :: Si $\in$ Ri)

M3: ($\forall$ i : $1 \leq$ i $\leq$ N :: |Ri | = K)

M4: Any site WSj is contained in K number of Ri s, $1 \leq$ i, j $\leq$ N.

Maekawa used projective planes theory and showed that $N = K(K - 1) + 1$. This relation gives |Ri | = $\sqrt{N}$.

- Conditions M1 and M2 are necessary for correctness; whereas M3 and M4 gives other features to the algorithm.
- Condition M3 states that requests set size of all sites should be equal implying that all sites must do equal work to invoke mutual exclusion.
- Condition M4 enforces that all sites have "equal responsibility" of granting permission to other sites, means same number of sites should request permission from any site.

The Algorithm

A site WSi executes the following steps to execute the CS:

Requesting the Critical Section

(a) A site WSi sends REQUEST(i) messages to all sites in its request set Ri in order to requests access to the CS.

(b) After receiving the REQUEST(i) message, site WSj sends a REPLY(j) message to WSi provided it has not sent a REPLY message to a site since its receipt of the last RELEASE message. Otherwise, it queues up the REQUEST(i) for later consideration.

Executing the Critical Section

(c)   Only after receiving a REPLY message from every site in WRi, site WSi executes the CS.

Releasing the Critical Section

(d)   Site WSi sends a RELEASE (i) message to every site in WRi after the completion of CS execution.

(e)   Site WSj after receiving a RELEASE (i) message from site WSi sends a REPLY message to the next site waiting in the queue and deletion of that entry from the queue takes place. If the queue is empty, then the site updates its state to show that no REPLY message has been not sent out since the receipt of the last RELEASE message.

Correctness

Theorem: Maekawa's algorithm achieves mutual exclusion.

Proof:

Proof is by contradiction. Suppose two sites WSi and WSj are executing the CS concurrently. This means all sites in WRi sends a REPLY message to site WSi and concurrently all sites in WRj sends a REPLY message to site WSj.

If WRi $\cap$ WRj = {Sk}, then site WSk must have sent REPLY messages concurrently to the sites WSi and WSj, which is a contradiction.

Performance

Since the size of a request set is $\sqrt{N}$, then CS execution requires $\sqrt{N}$ REQUEST, $\sqrt{N}$ REPLY, and $\sqrt{N}$ RELEASE messages, that results in 3"N messages per CS execution.

Synchronization delay of the algorithm is 2T because when a site WSi exits from the CS, firstly all the sites in WRi are released and then a REPLY message is sent by one of those sites to the next executing site for CS.

Test Your Progress

1.   Explain Lamport's non-token based algorithm.
2.   Explain Ricart-Agrawala algorithm.

4.6   Token Based Algorithm

All sites shares a unique token. A site having the token can only enter its CS. Instead of using timestamps these algorithms use sequence numbers.

4.6.1 Suzuki-Kasami's Broadcast Algorithm

A site not having token and still wants to enter the CS, then a REQUEST message is broadcasted for the token to all other sites. After receiving its REQUEST message, a site that possesses the token sends its token to the requesting site. If a site receives a REQUEST message while executing the CS, the token is sent only after the execution of the CS is completed.

The Algorithm

Requesting the Critical Section

(a) Requesting site WSi increments its sequence number RNi [i] if it does not have the token, and sends a REQUEST(i, sn) message to all other sites. ('sn' is the updated value of RNi [i].)

(b) After receiving this message, site WSj sets RNj [i] to max(RNj [i],sn). If WSj has the idle token, then the token is sent to WSi if RNj [i] = LN[i]+1.

Executing the Critical Section

(c) After receiving the token site, WSi executes the CS.

Releasing the Critical Section:

After finishing the execution of the CS, site WSi takes the following actions:

(d) LN[i] element of the token array is set equal to RNi [i].

(e) For every site WSj whose id is not in the token queue, it appends its id to the token queue if RNi [j] = LN[j]+1.

(f) After the above update if the token queue is non-empty, the top site id is deleted by WSi from the token queue and the token is sent to the site indicated by the id.

Correctness

Since there is single token in the system and during the CS execution the site holds the token, so mutual exclusion is guaranteed.

Theorem: A requesting site enters the CS in finite time T.

Proof:

In finite time T the token request messages of a site WSi reach to other sites. Since in finite time T one of these sites will have the token, so the request of site WSi will be placed in the token queue. In front of this request in the token queue there can be at most N – 1 requests, so site WSi will execute the CS after getting the token in finite time T.

Performance

If at the time T of its request a site holds the idle token, no message is required and the synchronization delay will be zero. While making a request if a site does not hold the token, the algorithm requires N messages for getting the token. Algorithm has synchronization delay of 0 or T.

4.6.2 Singhal's Heuristic Algorithm

Every site manages the state record of other sites and makes use of it to select a set of sites that can have the token. Site then requests the token from these sites only, hence reduces the messages required to execute the CS.

Data Structures

- A site WSi maintains two arrays, SVi [1..N] and SNi [1..N], to store the state and the sequence number(highest) for each site, respectively.

- The token also manages two such arrays as well (denoted by TSV[1..N] and TSN [1..N]). Sequence numbers detect the requests that are outdated.

- A site can be in one of the following states:

  R - Requesting the CS

  E - Executing the CS

  H - Holding the idle token

  N - None of the above

Initialization

For every sites WSi, i = 1,...,N do

{ SVi [j]: = N for j = N,...,i; SVi [j]: = R for j = i - 1,...,1;

SNi [j]: = 0 for j = 1,..., N}

Initially, site WS1 is in state H (i.e., WS1 [1]: = H).

For the token

{ TSV[j]: = N and TSN: = 0 for j = 1,...,N }

The Algorithm

Requesting the Critical Section

(a) If the requesting site WSi takes the following actions if it does not have the token:

- It sets SVi [i]: = R.

- It increments SNi [i]: = SNi [i]+1.

- It sends REQUEST(i, sn) message to all sites WSj for which

SVi [j] = R. (sn is the updated value of SNi [i].)

(b) After receiving the REQUEST(i, sn) message, site WSj discards the message if SNj [i] ≥ sn because the message is out of date. Otherwise, it sets SNj [i] to sn and takes the following actions based on its own state:

- SVj [j] = N: Set SVj [i]: = R.

- SVj [j] = R: If SVj [i] R, then Set SVj [i]: = R and send a REQUEST(j,SNj [j]) message to WSi (else do nothing).

- SVj [j] = E: Set SVj [i]: = R.

- SVj [j] = H: Set SVj [i]: = R, TSV[i]: = R, TSN [i]: = sn, SVj [j]: = N, and send the token to site WSi .

Executing the Critical Section

(c) WSi executes the CS after it has received the token. WSi sets SVi [i] to E before entering the CS.

Releasing the Critical Section

(d)   WSi sets SVi [i]: = N and TSV[i]: = N after finishing the execution of the CS, and updation of its local and token vectors takes place in the following way:

For all WSj , j = 1 to N do

    if SNi [j] > TSN [j]

then (* update token information from local information *)

    { TSV[j] : = SVi [j]; TSN [j] : = SNi [j] }

else (* update local information from token information *)

    { SVi [j] : = TSV[j]; SNi [j] : = TSN[j] }

(e)   If ($\forall$ j :: SVi [i] = N), then set SVi [i]: = H, else send the token to a site WSj such that SVi [j] = R.

4.6.3 Raymond's Tree-Based Algorithm

This algorithm uses a spanning tree for reducing the messages that are exchanged per critical section execution. Consider the network is as a graph, a tree under a network that contains all the N nodes is called a spanning tree. The algorithm assumes guarantee of message delivery under the network. All the network nodes are 'completely reliable. The algorithm operates on a minimal spanning tree of the network topology or a logical structure which is imposed on the network. The algorithm assumes the network nodes are already arranged in an unrooted tree structure. Figure 4.3 shows seven nodes of a spanning tree namely A, B, C, D, E, F, and G. Messages among nodes travels along the undirected edges of the tree.

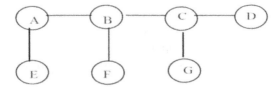

Figure 4.3: Seven Nodes of a Spanning Tree

A node holds the information about and communicates only to its immediate-neighbouring nodes. This algorithm uses a concept of privilege which is similar to token concept used in token-based algorithms,. At any time T only one node can be the privileged node, except when the privilege is in transit in the form of a PRIVILEGE message. When no node requests for the privilege, it remains in possession of the last used node.

The HOLDER Variables

A HOLDER variable is maintained by each node which provides information about the placement of the privilege in relation to the node itself. A node stores the identity of a node in its HOLDER variable that it thinks has the privilege. For two nodes X and Y, if HOLDERX = Y, we could redraw the undirected edge as a directed edge from X to Y. For instance, if G is the privileged node, Figure 4.3 can be redrawn with logically directed edges as shown in the Figure 4.4. In Figure 4.5 the shaded node represents the privileged node. For various nodes the values of the HOLDER variables will be the following:

HOLDERA = B

HOLDERB = C

HOLDERC = G

HOLDERD = C

HOLDERE = A

HOLDERF = B

HOLDERG = self

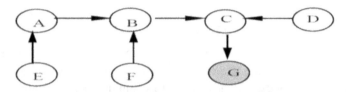

Figure 4.4: Appearance in Privileged Node G in a Tree

Figure 4.4 shows that tree is arranged with logically directed edges, all pointing in a direction towards node G - the privileged node.

Now suppose node B wants to execute the critical section which does not have the privilege. B sends a REQUEST message to the HOLDERB, i.e., C, which in turn forwards the REQUEST message to the HOLDERC, i.e., G. If the privileged node (G) no longer needs the privilege, then sends the PRIVILEGE message to its neighbour C, which made a request for the privilege, and resets HOLDERG to C as shown in Figure 4.5. Node C forwards the PRIVILEGE to node B, since it requested the privilege on behalf of B. Node C also resets HOLDERC to B. The tree in Figure 4.4 will now look as shown in Figure 4.5.

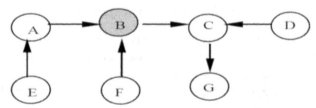

Figure 4.5: Appearance on Node B in the Spanning Tree

Mutual Exclusion

The algorithm ensures that only single node holds the privilege at any instant of time T. After receiving a PRIVILEGE message, that node becomes privileged. Similarly a node becomes unprivileged whenever it sends a PRIVILEGE message. There is no privileged node between the time T when one node becomes unprivileged and another node becomes privileged.

Deadlock is Impossible

A deadlock may occur when one or more nodes want to enter the critical section but fail to do so. This could happen due to any of the scenario given below:

1. The new node cannot be given privilege because of no already privileged node.
2. The privileged node is unaware that there are other nodes requesting the privilege.
3. Requesting unprivileged node does not get the PRIVILEGE message

Because nodes do not fail and there is no loss of messages, so scenario 1 can never occur. By using HOLDER variables the established logical pattern ensures that privilege needy node sends a REQUEST message either to a privileged node or to a node that has a path to a privileged node. So scenario 2 will not occur. The series of REQUEST messages are enqueued in the REQUEST Qs of various nodes which collectively provides a logical path for the transfer of the PRIVILEGE message. So scenario 3 can never occur.

Starvation is Impossible

When A is the privileged node, and node B requests for the privilege, the identity of B or the id's of proxy nodes for B will be present in the REQUEST Qs of all the nodes in the path connecting the requesting node and the current privileged node. Node B will receive the privilege which will depend upon the position of the id of node B in the REQUEST Qs. Node B will surely receive the privilege if its REQUEST message reaches the privileged node A.

Test Your Progress

1. What do you understand by Token-Based algorithms? Explain.
2. Explain Suzuki–Kasami's algorithm.

4.7 Comparative Performance Analysis of Token-Based and Non-Token Based Algorithm

4.7.1 Response Time

Response time increases in all mutual exclusion algorithms if the load is increased because contention for accessing the CS is increased. Depending on the load different algorithms see different increase in response time. There is no closed form expression of response time as a function of load exists for these algorithms.

4.7.2 Synchronization Delay

It is the time gap between a site leaves the CS and the next site enters the CS due to the sequential message exchanges. In most of the algorithms, a site that exits the CS directly sends a REPLY message or the token to the site entering the CS, which results in synchronization delay of T.

4.7.3 Message Traffic

Irrespective of the load the messages requirement per CS execution for The Lamport's, Ricart-Agrawala, and Suzuki-Kasami algorithms are 3*(N 1), 2*(N 1), and N respectively. In other algorithms, the required number of messages depends upon the load and is discussed below in Table 4.1.

Table 4.1: A Comparison of Performance (ll = light load, hl = heavy load) of Token-Based and Non-Token Based Algorithms

NON-TOKEN	Resp. time (ll)	Sync. Delay	Messages (ll)	Messages (hl)
Lamport	2T+E	T	3(N-1)	3(N-1)
Ricar-Arawala	2T+E	T	2(N-1)	2(N-1)
Maekawa	2T+E	2T	$3\sqrt{N}$	$5\sqrt{N}$
TOKEN	Resp. time (ll)	Sync. Delay	Messages (ll)	Messages (hl)
Suzuki and Kasami	2T+E	T	N	N
Singhal's Heuristic	2T+E	T	N/2	N
Raymond	T(log N)+E	T log(N)/2	log(N)	4

4.7.4 Universal Performance Bounds

Universal performance bounds can be determined for mutual exclusion algorithms. These bounds depend upon system characteristics, not upon any particular mutual exclusion algorithm.

Test Your Progress

1.   Compare and contrast token-based and non–token based algorithm.
2.   How can universal performance bounds be determined for mutual algorithms?

4.8   Summary

We know the problem of mutual exclusion frequently arises in distributed system whenever concurrent access to shared resources by several sites is involved. In this Chapter, we have learned various token and non-token based algorithms to remove mutual exclusion in our distributed system. We learned a good comparison between these various algorithms.

4.9 Key Terms

- **Algorithm:** A step-by-step procedure for calculations.
- **Deadlock:** A situation in which two or more competing actions are to be processed and each waiting for the other to finish but neither ever does.
- **FIFO:** First In, First Out; a method used to organize and manipulate a data stack, where the first entry or bottom of the stack is processed first.
- **Mutual exclusion:** Mutex; a program object that prevents simultaneous access to a shared resource.
- **Spanning tree:** A network protocol that ensures a loop-free topology for any

bridged Ethernet local area network.

- **Starvation:** A problem encountered in multitasking where a process is perpetually denied necessary resources.

4.10 Exercise

1. Define distributed mutual exclusion. What are the requirements of mutual exclusion algorithms.

2. Explain the classification of distributed mutual exclusion.

3. Differentiate between token based and non-based algorithms.

4. Discuss Maekawa's algorithm.

5. Discuss Singhal's Heuristic algorithm.

6. Describe Raymond's tree–based algorithm.

7. What are the universal performance bounds?

8. What do you mean by problem of mutual exclusion in distributed system? What are the requirements of a good mutual exclusion algorithm?

9. Explain the performance matrices to judge the performance of distributed mutual exclusion algorithm.

Chapter 5
Distributed Deadlock Detection

5.1   Introduction

A deadlock is a main problem in distributed systems. A process may request resources, while that resource is held by other processes. If the chain of the assignment of resources to the processor is not verified properly, deadlock can occurs. We can say that deadlock is a special state where a set of processes P's request resources R's that are held by other processes in the set.

5.1.1 Necessary Condition

A deadlocks situation can arise if all of the following conditions hold simultaneously in a system:

- **Mutual Exclusion:** In mutual exclusion at least one resource must be held in a non-shareable mode. Only one process can use one resource at any given instant of time.

- **Hold and Wait:** A process P is holding at least one resource R and requesting for other resources that are held by some other processes.

- **No Preemption:** The Distributed system must not de-allocate resources R's once they have been allocated; they must be released by the holding process P voluntarily an add into a list of resources.

- **Circular Wait:** In a circular wait, the process P must be waiting for completion of other processes or resource which is being held by another process P1, P2,... etc, which in turn is waiting for the first process P to release the resource R. In general, there is a set of waiting processes, P = {P1, P2, ..., PN}, such that PN is waiting for a resource held by P1, P1 is waiting for a resource held by P2 and so on until P(N-1) is waiting for a resource held by PN.

5.1.2 Distributed Deadlock

Deadlock is a state in which a set of process is waiting for resources that are held by some other processes. It describes by four basic requirements: Mutual Exclusion, Hold and wait, No Preemption and Circular wait. It is very easy to detect whether system is centralized or on single computer/system.

Distributed Deadlock is a state in which set of processes (here individual process is on different sites/servers/system) are waiting for resources that are held by some other processes on multiple sites. Due to processes running on multiple sites is very difficult to identify, avoid and prevent deadlock in distributed system. We can use following techniques for handling Deadlock:

- **Deadlock Ignorance:** ignore the deadlock and assume that deadlock did not occur.

- **Deadlock Detection:** when deadlock occurs, identify deadlock and solve it by abort/terminate the few processes or restart the processes.

- **Deadlock Prevention:** we prevent the deadlock only by to prevent the one of four primary conditions does not hold.

- **Deadlock Avoidance:** Before assigning a new resource must be checked safe and unsafe situation. Assign the resources only when system will be in a safe state.

Test Your Progress

1. Define the following terms:
   i. Deadlock
   ii. Distributed deadlock
   iii. Global deadlock
2. List necessary conditions for deadlock.

5.2 Preliminaries

5.2.1 System Model

Distributed system model is set of n processes (p1, p2 ...pn) in asynchronous mode, which communicate with each other by message passing.

In this model each process running on different processor, which does not share global memory with other processes and communicate individually by message passing over the communication network.

We make the following assumptions:

- The systems/process has only reusable resources.
- Processes/systems are allowed to make only exclusive access to resources.
- There is only one copy of each resource.

5.2.2 Resource Versus Communication Deadlock

Resource Deadlocks

A process may many resources for performed an activity. In resource deadlock, if processes are waiting for resources held by another process P in the same set {P1, P2 ...PN}, then it must receive all the requested resources to execute a task.

Communication Deadlocks

Processes wait for communication medium to communicate with other processes in the set. In communication deadlock, each process waits to communicate with another process among sets of processes. In the set, process is waiting for another process's message S, and no process in the set initiates a message S until it receives a message for which it is waiting for.

5.2.3 Graph Theoretic Model
Wait-for Graph

When one process requests for the resource and that resources is held by other processes, this sequence made a circular graph.

Wait-for Graphs (WFG): P1 -> P2 implies P1 which is waiting for a resource from P2. In a WFG, nodes are processes and there is a directed edge from node P1 to Resource R1 ,R1 held by Process P2. if P1 is blocked then is waiting for P2 to release same resource R1

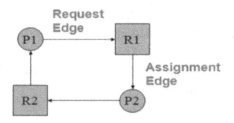

Figure 5.1: Wait-for Graph (WFG)

Test Your Progress
1. Explain the terms:
    i.   Resource deadlock
    ii.   Communication deadlock
2. What do you mean by resource allocation graph?
3. What is Wait-for-Graph?

5.3   Deadlock Handling Strategies

5.3.1 Deadlock Prevention

Deadlock prevention is achieved by having a process collect all the needed resources at once before it begins executing or by preempting a process that holds the needed resource. This approach is highly incompetent and unrealistic in distributed systems.

5.3.2 Deadlock Avoidance

For deadlock avoidance in distributed systems, we use the approach that a resource is assigned to a process if state of global system is safe. State of global system includes all processes and resources in distributed system.

5.3.3 Deadlock Detection

Deadlock detection requires status of the process and resources interactions for availability of cyclic wait. The best approach for deadlock handling in distributed system is deadlock detection.

Test Your Progress:
1. What is deadlock prevention? Explain.
2. What is deadlock detection? Explain.
3. What are the advantages and disadvantages of deadlock avoidance?
4. Explain different methods of deadlock handling strategies.

5.4 Deadlock Detection and Resolution Issues

Deadlock detection and resolution issues, address two basic issues; first, **detection of existing deadlocks** and second, **resolution of detected deadlocks.**

Detection

Generally detection of deadlock is maintained by two basic issues: maintains of WFG and Detection of presence of WFG cycle. In distributed system, a cycle may involve several site/processors. Depending on multiple sites which maintain the information about WFG, we search for WFG including several sites information. There are various algorithms for deadlock detection; centralized, distributed and hierarchical.

In distributed system, it is very difficult to design a correct algorithm for deadlock detection because sites may maintain outdated data and inconsistent WFG's of the system.

Resolution

Deadlock resolution involves breaking existing wait for dependencies in the system WFG to resolve the deadlock. It involves rolling back one or more steps that are created deadlocks and assigning their resources to blocked processes in the deadlock so that they can resume their execution when complete system is deadlock free.

5.5 Control Organization for Distributed Deadlock Detection

5.5.1 Centralized Control

- An elected site known as the *control site* is responsible for constructing and maintaining the global WFG and also search for cycles. Following are the features of an elected site:
  - ➢ Single point of failure.
  - ➢ High message traffic to and from the control site.
  - ➢ Message traffic is independent of the rate of deadlock formation.
- Site's are request for resource and release resources including local resources, by sending request resource and release resource messages to the control site.
- Control site updates its WFG after receiving messages from other sites and checks for deadlock.

5.5.2 Distributed Control

All sites together cooperate to detect a cycle in the state graph that is likely to be distributed over several sites of the system. Deadlock detection is started whenever a process is forced to wait.

5.5.3 Hierarchical Control

Sites are orderly arranged in a hierarchical fashion and the site is responsible for detecting deadlocks involving only its children sites.

Test Your Progress

1. Name the two basic issues which are addressed by deadlock detection and resolution techniques.
2. Explain centralized control algorithm
3. Explain distributed control algorithm
4. What is hierarchical control?

5.6 Centralized Deadlock Detection Algorithm

5.6.1 Completely Centralized Algorithm

It is a very simple centralized deadlock detection algorithm, in which a designated site is called control site, maintain the WFG of the entire system and checks it for existence of deadlock cycles. All sites request and release resources by sending request resources and release request message respectively to the control site. Whenever control site receives a request for resources or release resources message, it will correspondingly update the WFG. The control site checks WFG for deadlocks whenever a request edge is added to WFG. This algorithm is conceptually very simple and easy to implement but unfortunately this is highly inefficient because all resources acquired and release request must go through the control site, even when the resources are on local site. It will result in large delay in responding local requests, large communication overhead and may be a congestion of communication links near the control site.

5.6.2 Ho-Ramamoorthy Algorithm

The Two-phase Algorithm

- Each site maintains a status table which contain the status of all the processes started at that site.
  - ➢ Resources are locked.
  - ➢ Resources are being waited for.
- At regular intervals, the elected site requests the status table from all sites, constructs a WFG from the information received and searches it for cycles.
- If the cycle is detected, the designated site again requests status tables from all the sites and again constructs a WFG using only those transactions that are common to both reports to see if the same cycle is detected again. If it happens, the control site will declare the system to be deadlocked.
- The elected site reduces the probability of getting a not consistent state of the system and reporting false deadlock.

The One-phase Algorithm

- Every site maintains two status tables.
  - ➢ A resource status table.
  - ➢ A process status table.
- Every so often, a designated site requests both the tables from every site,

constructs a WFG using only those transactions for which the entry in the resource table matches the equivalent entry in the process table, and searches the WFG for cycles.

> ➢ No false deadlocks detected.

- Evaluation of the two-phase and one-phase algorithm.

  > ➢ One-phase is faster.
  > ➢ Requires fewer messages.

Test Your Progress

1. Explain completely centralized algorithm with the help of example.
2. Explain one–phase and two–phase algorithms.

5.7 Distributed Deadlock Detection Algorithm

Distributed Deadlock Detection (DDD) algorithm can be divided into four classes: path pushing, edge chasing, diffusion computation and global state detection. Let us discuss each of them in brief.

In the path pushing, we are calculating wait for dependency information of global WFG. Global WFG is designed with the help of sequence of wait for dependency edge. In edge chasing algorithm, we use a unique message called *probe*, which circulated along the edges of global WFG to detect a cycle.

5.7.1 Path Pushing Algorithm

Distributed deadlocks are detected only when we find global WFG. The fundamental idea is to build a global WFG for each site of the distributed system. At each site WS whenever deadlock detection is performed, it sends its local Wait-for Graph (WFG) to all the adjacent sites WS's. After the local data structure of each site WS is updated, this updated WFG is then passed along to other sites WS's, and the procedure is repeated until some site WS has an adequately complete graph of the global state to identify deadlock or to establish that deadlocks are not present. This characteristic of a distribution around the paths of global WFG has lead to the term path-pushing algorithms.

5.7.2 Edge Chasing Algorithm

In an edge-chasing algorithm, the availability of a cycle in a Wait-for Graph is identified by propagating special messages called probes S, along the edges of the graph. Probe messages are unlike than the request and reply messages. The construction of cycle can be deleted by the site WS if it receives the matching probe message S sent by it previously. Whenever a process P that is executing receives a probe message S, it rejects this message S and continues. Just blocked processes propagate probe messages along their outgoing edges. Main benefit of edge-chasing algorithm is that probes are fixed size messages which are usually very short.

5.7.3 Diffusion Computation-Based Algorithm

For distributed deadlock detection algorithm like diffusion computation; deadlock detection computation is diffused through the Wait-for Graph of the system. Such algorithms must use echo algorithms for detecting deadlocks. This computation is imposed on the underlying distributed diffusion-based computation. If this computation will terminate, the initiator will declare a deadlock. For identifying a deadlock, a process P sends out query messages S along all the outgoing edges in the Wait-for Graph. These queries messages are successively propagated (i.e., diffused) through the edges of the WFG. When a blocked process P receives first query information for a particular deadlock detection initiation, it does not send a reply message S until it has received a reply message S for every query it has already sent. For all subsequent queries for this deadlock detection initiation, it immediately sends back a reply message S. The initiator of deadlock detection detects a deadlock when it receives a reply for every query it had sent out.

5.7.4 Global State Detection-Based Algorithm

Global State (GS) detection-based deadlock detection algorithm has the following ponits:

➢ A consistent snapshot of a Distributed System (DS) can be obtained without freezing the underlying computation.

➢ If a stable property holds in the system before the snapshot collection is initiated, this property will still hold in the snapshot.

Therefore, distributed deadlocks can be detected by taking a snapshot of the system and examining it for the condition of a deadlock.

Test Your Progress

1. Name the four classes of DDD algorithm.
2. What do you mean by global state detection-based algorithm? Explain.
3. What is edge chasing algorithm?
4. Explain diffusion computation-based algorithm.

5.8 Hierarchical Deadlock Detection Algorithms

5.8.1 Menasce-Muntz Algorithm

In this algorithm, all the controllers are arranged in the tree fashion. The controller at the bottom most level manages resources and others are responsible for deadlock detection.

Whenever a change occurs in a controllers Transaction Wait-for Graph (TWF) due to resources allocation, wait or release, it is propagated to its parent controller. The parent controller makes changes in its TWF graph, searches for cycle, and propagates the changes upward, if necessary. A non-leaf controller can receive up-to-date information concerning the TWF graph of its children continuously or periodically.

5.8.2 Ho-Ramamoorthy Algorithm

In this algorithm, sites are grouped into several disjoint clusters, in which a site chosen as central control site or head of clusters head, which dynamically chosen control site/cluster head for each cluster head. The central control site requests from every control site their inter-cluster transaction status information and wait for relations.

Consequently, a control site collects status table from all the sites in its cluster and applies the one-phase deadlock detection algorithm to detect all deadlock involving only inter-cluster transactions. So it will send inter-cluster information status information and wait for relation to the central control site. Thus the central site detects all deadlocks located in its cluster, and the central control site detects all inter-cluster deadlocks.

5.9   Summary

In this Chapter we have learned that how deadlock occurs in a distributed system. As we know that deadlock detection is a major concern to maintain a deadlock free system, in this Chapter we have also learned that how to detect deadlock in a distributed system and how to resolve that problem in a distributed system.

5.10   Key Terms

● **Communication network:** A collection of terminal nodes, links and any intermediate nodes which are connected to enable telecommunication between the terminals.

● **Edge chasing**: An algorithm for deadlock detection in distributed systems.

● **Path pushing**: An algorithm which is used to build a global wait-for graph for each site of the distributed system.

● **Wait-for graph**: A directed graph used for deadlock detection in operating systems and relational database systems.

5.11   Exercise

1.   What do you mean by deadlock?

2.   Differentiate between communication and resources deadlock.

3.   Explain the Ho-Ramamoorthy algorithm.

4.   What are the advantages and disadvantages of centralized deadlock detection?

Practice with Ease for Examination

1.   What do you mean by problem of mutual exclusion in distributed system? What are the requirements of a good mutual exclusion algorithm? How does the performance of a distributed algorithm evaluated?   (2007-08)

    See Section 4.3

2.   What are the token and non-token based algorithms? Explain Lamport's algorithm with example.   (2007-08)

    See Sections 4.5 and 4.6

3.   Explain the deadlock handling strategies in distributed system.   (2007-08)

    See Section 5.3

4.   Explain the control organization for distributed deadlock detection. (2007-08)
     See Section 5.5

5.   A centralized global deadlock detector holds the union of local wait-for graphs.
     Give an example to explain how a phantom deadlock could be detected if a
     waiting transaction in a deadlock cycle abort during deadlock detection
     procedure.   (2007-08)
     See Sections 5.3, 5.5

6.   What are the shortcomings of Ramamoorthy's two-phase algorithm for deadlock
     detection?   (2007-08)
     See Sections 5.6, 5.8

7.   What do you mean by problem of mutual exclusion in distributed system? What
     are the requirements of a good mutual exclusion algorithm? Explain the
     performance matrices to judge the performance of distributed mutual exclusion
     algorithm.   (2008-09)
     See Sections 5.1, 5.2, and 5.3

8.   What is the problem of distributed deadlock detection? What are the differences
     in centralized, distributed and hierarchical control organizations for distributed
     deadlock detection? What are advantages of distributed control organization
     over centralized control organization for distributed deadlock detection?

                                                                                   (2008-09)

     See Sections 5.3, 5.6

9.   What are the differences in centralized and distributed algorithms? How does
     the performance of a distributed algorithm evaluated? Explain the term 'message
     complexity' in reference to distributed algorithm.   (2008-09)
     See Sections 5.6, 5.7

10. Differentiate between token-based and non-token based algorithm.   (2009-10)
     See Sections 4.5, 4.6

11. Explain the classification of distributed mutual exclusion.   (2009-10)
     See Section 4.2

12. Define deadlock. Differentiate between resource and communication deadlocks.
     Discuss various deadlock handling strategies in detail.   (2009-10)
     See Section 5.2

13. Write short note on Wait–for graph.   (2009-10)
     See Section 5.2

14. Approaches based on shared variable (like semaphore) are not applicable to
     achieve mutual exclusion in distributed system. State whether this statement is
     correct or not and give the reason behind it.   (2011-12)
     See Section 5.3

15. Explain the Ricart-Agrawala algorithm for mutual exclusion. How many
     messages per critical section execution is required? (Assume there are N sites)
                                                                                   (2011-12)

     See Section 4.5.2

16. Suppose all the processes in the system are assigned priorities that can be used to totally order the processes. Modify edge chasing algorithm (Chandy's algorithm) so that when a process detects a deadlock it also knows the lowest priority deadlocked processes. (2011-12)

    See Section 5.7

17. Discuss the following: (2011-12)

    i.   Performance metric for distributed mutual exclusion algorithm.

    ii. Obermarck's path pushing algorithm.

    See Sections 5.6, 5.7

18. What is distributed mutual exclusion and briefly explain the requirements of mutual exclusion algorithms. (2011-12)

    See Sections 4.2, 4.3

19. Explain the various hierarchal deadlock detection algorithms with the help of suitable examples. Also compare the performance of various algorithms.

    (2011-12)

    See Section 5.8

20. What is the importance of different types of graph in deciding deadlock? What is the interactive consistency problem? (2011-12)

    See Sections 5.6,5.8

21. What is deadlock? What are the necessary conditions for occurrence of deadlock in distributed system? Describe the deadlock handling strategies in distributed system. (2012-13)

    See Sections 5.1, 5.2 and 5.3

22. Classify deadlock detection algorithm. Describe path pushing deadlock detection algorithm. (2012-13)

    See Section 5.7

23. Write and explain a token-based algorithm for mutual exclusion. Describe its performance on important metrics. (2012-13)

    See Section 4.6

24. What is mutual exclusion? Describe the importance of mutual exclusion in distributed system. Is mutual exclusion problem more complex in distributed system than single computer system? Justify your answer. (2013-14)

    See Section 5.6

25. What do you mean by deadlock avoidance? Explain in brief. Describe Edge-chasing deadlock detection algorithm. (2013-14)

    See Section 5.3

26. Write and explain a non-token based mutual exclusion algorithm. Describe its merits and demerits. (2013-14)

    See Section 4.5

Unit–III

Agreement Protocols: Introduction, System models, classification of Agreement Problem, Byzantine agreement problem, Consensus problem, Interactive consistency Problem, Solution to Byzantine Agreement problem, Application of Agreement problem, Atomic Commit in Distributed Database system.

Distributed Resource Management: Issues in distributed File Systems, Mechanism for building distributed file systems, Design issues in Distributed Shared Memory, Algorithm for Implementation of Distributed Shared Memory.

Chapter 6
Agreement Protocol

6.1 Introduction

When system is free from failure, an agreement can easily be reached among the processor or site. Processor can reach an agreement by communicating their value to reach other and then by taking a majority vote or a minimum, maximum, mean, etc., of those values. When the system is prone to failure this method does not work. This is because faulty processor can send conflicting values to other processors preventing them from reaching an agreement. In this chapter you will learn about agreement problems and their solutions.

6.2 System Model

6.2.1 Synchronous Versus Asynchronous Computation

Synchronous computation, model specifies that the process in the system executes step-by-step. The process receives a message for computing task performs the computation task and then forward the message to any other process for further computation. In the way, the computation task is performed step-by-step and one step is known as round. The messages are received and processed one after another. If there is any delay between messages then all computation work will be shut down and decrease the performance of system.

In asynchronous computation model, it is not necessary to perform the computation task in steps. The computation can be performed at any time without any sequence of steps.

6.2.2 Model of Processor Failure

In this model failure specifies in what way a faulty processor can behave.

- **Crash Failure:** A faulty processor stops prematurely and does nothing from that point on before stopping, however, it behaves correctly.

- **Send Omission:** Processor omits to send message to same processors. For example, a processor is supposed to broadcast the message to all other processors, but it sends the message to only few processors.

- **Receive Omission:** Processor omits to receive message sent to it.

- **Arbitrary failure:** Also known as Byzantine failure/ malicious failure. Processor can exhibit any behaviour whatsoever. For example to other processor to confuse them.

6.2.3 Authenticated Versus Non-Authenticated Messages

We known that distributed system works with the help of message exchange between site/processor and their processing. There are two types of messages:

- **Authentication Messages:** Authentication messages are not allowed to change by the faulty processor. The faulty processor can receive such messages and verify its authentication and then transfer it to others. Due to this only feature authenticated message are also called *"Signed Messages"*.

- **Non-authenticated Messages:** The faulty processor can change the content of non-authenticated message before it relays the message to other processors. Due to this feature non-authenticated message is also known as *"Oral Messages"*.

6.2.4 Performance Aspects

For evaluating performance, following parameters are used:

- **Time and Message Traffic:** No of message exchanges/ rounds needed to single value agreement.

- **Storage Overhead:** Amount of data that needs to saved at processors during execution of the agreement protocol.

Test Your Progress

1. Compare synchronous and asynchronous computation.
2. Explain the model of Processor failures.
3. Differentiate between authenticated and non-authenticated messages.

6.3   Classification of Agreement Problems

6.3.1 Byzantine Agreement Protocol

This protocol is based on an initial value generated by any processor. The processor which is used to initialize the value known as *source processor*. This processor broadcasts its value to all other processors in the system. This protocol requires one common value for getting the agreement. The following two are the main objection of the solution of this protocol.

- **Agreement:** All the non-faulty processor must be agree on one value.
- **Validity:** If the source processor is non faulty the it's initial value is used as agreement value. But this common value is not known to any faulty processor.

Problem

When processors are geographically dispersed then it is very difficult that all processors are agreeing on same agreement value that no conflict will occur after commitment. So they may not be able to reach agreement for at least one of the following reasons:

1. The agreement value message from one processor to another processor may be unable to deliver.
2. May be processor is faulty and not be able to reach one value.
3. If processor is faulty, it will send different value to other processor.

   The solution of this problem should follow the following condition:

1. All non-faulty processor should agree on same value.
2. If source is not faulty, then value initiated by source is final agreement value.
3. If source is faulty, the all non-faulty processor can agree on any arbitrary value.

6.3.2 Consensus Problem

According to this problem every processor broadcast its value to all other processor. Initial value of the processor may be different. A protocol for reaching consensus should meet the following condition:

- **Agreement:** all non-faulty processor agree on same single value.
- **Validity:** If the initial value of every non-faulty processor is **u** then the agreed value by all non-faulty processor must be **u**.

6.3.3 Interactive Consistency Problem

In interactive consistency problem, every processor broadcast its initial value to all other processors and all other processors broadcast their initial value to other processors.

The initial value of the processor may be different. A protocol for the interactive consistency problem should meet the following condition:

- **Agreement:** All non-faulty processor agree on the same vector (v1,v2,v3....vn).
- **Validity:** if the ith processor is non-faulty, mark its initial value is vi then the ith value to be agreed on by all non-faulty processor must be vi.

6.3.4 Relationship among the Agreement Problems

As previous discussion we say that if all non-faulty processor select a single common value then we reach to agreement. And if Byzantine agreement removed safely, then other problems will not arise. Because as we know in consensus agreement protocol problem is an extension of Byzantine problem if single value reaches to common value then consensus problem will not arise as same as with interactive protocol problem will arise.

Test Your Progress

1. Explain different classification of agreement problems.
2. What is Byzantine agreement problem?

6.4 Solution to Byzantine Agreement Problem

6.4.1 Upper Bound on the Number of Faulty Processors

For finding a solution for Byzantine problem, Pease says that number of Faulty processor M is not greater than (N-1)/3, where N is total number of processor. So we can say that,

$$M <= (N-1)/3$$

6.4.2 Impossibility Result

If a fully connected network of processor or sites is there, Pease says that we cannot reach to an agreement if number of faulty processor M is greater than (N-1)/3.

6.4.3 Lamport-Shostak-Pease Algorithm

This algorithm is based on Oral Message Algorithm OM (M), where M is total number of faulty processors, and 'N' = Number of processors and "N>= 3M+1". Algorithm is recursively defined as follows:

Algorithm OM (0)

1. Source processors send their values to every processor.
2. Every processor uses the value it receives from source and '0', used as default value for every processor if value is not received.

Algorithm OM (M), M>0

1. The source processor sends its value to each processor.
2. For every i, let Pi be the value for processor i receives from source and '0' used as default value for every processor if value is not received.
3. Processor i acts as the new source and initiates algorithm OM (M-1) where it sends the value Pi to each of the 'N-2' other processors.
4. For each i and j (not i), let Pj be the value for processor i received from processor j in Step 3. Processor i uses the value majority (P1, P2....Pn-1).

"The function majority (P1, P2....Pn-1) computes the majority value if exists otherwise it uses default value 0."

Test Your Progress

1. What are the solutions for Byzantine agreement problem?
2. Explain Lamport-shostak-pease algorithm.

6.5 Application of Agreement Algorithm

An algorithm for agreement problems finds applications in problem where processor should reach an agreement regarding their value in the presence of malicious failure. Two such applications are as follows:

1.   Fault Tolerant Clocks Synchronization

2.   Atomic Commit in Distributed Database System

6.5.1 Fault-Tolerant Clock Synchronization

In distributed system, it is often necessary that sites maintain physical clocks have a drift problem. They must be periodically synchronized. Such periodic synchronization becomes extremely difficult if the Byzantine failures are allowed.

This is because a faulty processor can report different clock value to different processors. The following assumptions regarding system are as follows:

- **Assumption 1:** All clocks are initially synchronized to approximately same value.

- **Assumption 2:** Non-faulty processors clocks run at approximately correct rate.

- **Assumption 3:** Non-Faulty process can read the clock value of another non-faulty process with at most a small error.

A clock synchronization algorithm should satisfy the following two conditions:

1.   At any time, the value of the clock of all non-faulty processor must be approximately equal.

2.   There is a small bound on the amount by which the clock of a non-faulty processor is changed during each resynchronization.

6.5.2 Atomic Commit in Distributed Database System

In the problem of atomic, sites of a distributed database system must agree whether commit or about a transaction. In the first phase of the atomic commit, sites execute their part of a distributed transaction and broadcast their decision to all other sites.

In the second phase, each site based on what it received from other sites in the first phase, decide whether to commit, or abort its part of the distributed computation since every site receives an identical response from all other sites, they can send conflicting response other sites, causing them to make conflicting decision.

In this situation, use algorithm for the Byzantine agreement to reach common decision.

A.   A common decision regarding sites works as per Byzantine agreement. Every sites execute their part of distributed transaction and broadcast their decision (commit or abort) to all other sites.

B.   Each site decides whether to commit or abort its part of distributed transaction based what it has received from other sites in the first phase.

Since every site receives an identical response from all other sites, they will reach the same decision.

But if some sites behave maliciously, they can send a conflicting response to other sites, causing them to make conflicting decision. In this situation we can use

Byzantine agreement to ensure that all non-faulty processors reach a common decision about a distributed transaction.

Test Your Progress

1.   What are the applications of agreement algorithms?

2.   What is interactive convergence?

6.6   Summary

Agreement problem arises in every distributed system whether it is distributed database system, distributed system or any other. Byzantine is unique and only solution for any type of distributed system. Pease gives us a solution for Byzantine protocol problem which will remove other two problems also, Consensus and Interactive consistency problem.

6.7   Key Terms

●   **Clock synchronization algorithm:** A problem from computer science and engineering which deals with the idea that internal clocks of several computers may differ.

●   **Oral message:** Non-authenticated message.

●   **Storage overhead:** Amount of data that needs to saved at processors during execution of the agreement protocol.

6.8   Exercise

1.   What do you understand by Agreement problem?

2.   How we will remove Agreement protocol problems?

3.   Discuss the general system model where agreement protocols are used.

4.   Explain the Byzantine agreement problem and agreement and validity condition for it.

5.   Show that Byzantine agreement cannot always be reached among four processor if two of them are faulty.

Chapter 7
Distributed File System

7.1 Introduction

A distributed file system is necessary component of distributed operating system. It uses different types of technique to share file between all autonomous computer systems. Distributed File System (DFS) used for sharing of stored data is possibly the most important aspect of distributed sharing. DFS also provides redundancy and location transparency to improve data availability in case of failures. Using DFS we allow to users to share physically distributed computers information and sharing resources by using a common file system. DFS is a collection of computers and workstations connected by LAN (Local Area Network). It is implemented as part of the operating system of each of the connected computers. A DFS maintains network transparency. It means the availability of the file distributed over the network in the same way the file residing at one location.

7.1.1 Goal of Distributed File System:

Resource Sharing

The popularity of computer system arises due to nature of some applications. In such cases, it is necessary to facilitate sharing long-storage devices and their data to make system more user friendly.

Transparency

The main functionality of DFS is transparency which means user would be unaware about data location, movement, access, etc.

High Availability

The main feature of DFS is high availability. This feature states that if one server goes offline or failure, the data stored on its hard drives is still available for other nodes.

Location Independence

File name should not be changed when its physical location changes.

User Mobility

Access to file from anywhere or from any remote location.

Test Your Progress

1. What do you mean by file system?
2. List the goals of distributed file system.

7.2 Distributed File System Architecture

In DFS, files are stored at any machine and computations perform by any machine (i.e., the machine are the peers). The remote machine performs the necessary file access operation and returns data if a read operation is performed successfully. However, for higher performance several machines, known as *file servers*, are committed to store files or data and retrieve information. The rest of the machines in system can be used slowly for computational purposes. These machines are referred to as clients and they access those files which are stored on servers as shown in Figure 7.1. Some clients machines may also be equipped with a local storage that can be performed caching for remote files, as a data or file swap area, or as a storage place. The two most essential services used in distributed file system are: name server and cache manager. Let us discuss each of these services in brief.

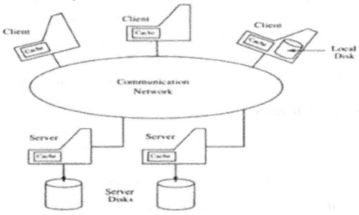

Figure 7.1: Clients and Servers Setup

Name Server: A name server is a process which maps name specified by clients to the stored objects, such as file and directories. The mapping occurs when a process running a file or directory for the first time.

Cache Manager: A cache manager is the process that implements caching. In a file caching a copy of data stored at remote file server is brought to the client machine when accessed by the client. Subsequent access to the data is performed locally at the client thereby reducing the accessed delay due to network latency. If multiple clients are allowed to cache a file and modify it the copy becomes not consistent. To avoid this problem, a cache manager at both ends servers and clients, coordinates to perform data storage and retrieval operation. Typically how data proceeds in DFS shown in Figure 7.2.

When processor sends request for a data block first it checks into local cache if not found then, it will check in local disk. If data block is not available in local system or client machine. Then the request is passed to a file server (as determined by Name server) as shown in Figure 7.2. Server check data block in the cache and disk for transferring it to client machine. Data block must be available before issuing disk I/O (Input/Output) request.

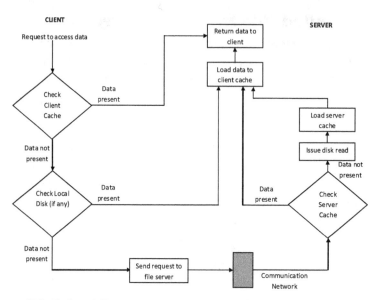

Figure 7.2: Role of Communication Network between Clients and Servers

Test Your Progress

1. Define:
    i.   Cache Manager
    ii. Name Server
2. Explain the architecture of distributed file system.

7.3   Design Issues in Distributed File System

We describe the various design issues in distributed file system. After discussion main design issue in distributed file system is:

7.3.1 Naming and Name Resolution

Naming is a mapping scheme generally done between logical and physical object. For example, user deals with logical data object represented by files name, whereas the system manipulates physical block of data, stored on disk. Usually a client refers to file by textual name, which is mapped to lower numerical identifiers that, in turn, map to a disk block.

Advantages

● Unique file name facility.
● Name resolution technique is simple as file can be easily found.

Limitations

● It will conflict with the objective of network transparency.
● When we move file from one site to another site, there is need to change file name and applications which will access the file.

7.3.2 Cache on Disk or Main Memory

The benefits obtained by employing file caches at client are known to us. Now we are concerned with the question of whether the data cached by client should be main memory at the client end.

Advantages

- Caching advantage gained by workstations are diskless.
- It is faster than access data from local disk.
- Same design for caching is used for server and client.

Limitations

- Caching large files will not affect the system performance.
- Implements virtual memory management.
- Distributed system is also incorporated with portable workstation.

7.3.3 Writing Policy

Writing policy is decided when modified cache should be transferred from server to client or from client to server. Following policies are used:

1. **Write Through:** According to this policy the request made by the client is carried to server immediately. In this way, the server keeps all updated data which will fulfil all client requests. This policy is important to the client request and if system is crashed, the information of client request remains on the main server.

2. **Delayed Writing Policy:** This policy is concerned with the delay of writing server when the data is modified and the modification is reflected to server after time delay. The data block is modified and kept in local centre of client, and after many writes this block is transferred to server. These intermediate results are not stored to server because they are deleted from local cache.

3. **Write on Close Policy:** This policy delays the updating of files on the server side because the files are not closed at the client sides. It means the client updates the file locally and then goes to process. Then the server updates file.

7.3.4 Cache Consistency

The problems of cache consistency arise when many of the clients cache share same data and want to modify the shared data. So we need a guarantee the consistency of the client system. The two types of approaches used to maintain cache consistency are:

1. **Server-initiated Approach:** In this approach server is responsible for informing cache manager about valid data block. The data in the client cache becomes invalid, server informs cache manager of client side then the cache manager of client can retrieve new data. The information is initiated by server system.

2. **Client-initiated Approach:** This approach is related with cache manager at the client side is responsible for data invalidation. The validity of data is checked with the server before returning it to the client.

7.3.5 Availability

To provide availability to the client, replication is a primary solution for it.

Availability is destroyed due to server failure or communication link failures.

Replication

Replication is a primary approach to provide availability of files or data to the client or server. In this approach, many replicas are maintained at multiple servers.

Limitations

- Multiple replicas increase the storage space.
- Maintenance of multiple replicas is an extra overhead.
  Following are the reasons to increase inconsistency among replicas:
- All replicas are not updated regularly due to server failure.
- Due to communication failure some of the replicas sever will not be reachable.

Unit of Replication: To maintain replicas following units are designed.

(a) **The most basic unit is file:** In this approach, only some of files are under replication, which need higher availability. Protection rights are associated with all replicas directory. Each directory may not use common name so extra name resolution is required to locate with each replica in case of modification of directory or files is to be done.

(b) **Group of files called volumes can be used:** In this unit, we maintain volume, which is known as group of files on servers. This approach uses a code file system scheme, in which protection rights are associated with each volume. Sometimes this approach is wasteful when client requires only few files from the volume.

(c) **Combination of volume and single file replication can be used:** In this approach, we use primary pack, in which all the files of a client form a files group. Primary pack replica is called a *pack*, which contains a subset of files from primary pack. One or more pack can be form from primary pack as client requirement.

7.3.6 Scalability

In this design issue, we maintain a DFS, such as to increase the number of flies, number of clients, number of servers, number of replica, etc., as per our need and also for future requirements.

As per DFS future requirements when system grows in both the size of a severs state and load on the server.

Following steps we will follow to reduce server state and server load:

(a) Increase the number files in read only mode so that we will need not to check validation of files.

(b) Sometimes data is required by one client can reside another client's cache rather than server.

So we can say that structure of a server plays a main role in DFS system. If server is designed with single process, then many clients have to wait for a long time whenever a disk input/output is initiated. This can be avoided if separate process is assigned to each client.

7.3.7 Semantics

Accessing of files can affect due to semantic of a DFS. The common semantic is that read operation fetches data due to updated write operation. In this approach all read and write must be go through the server. Sharing of files is not allowed, when multiple writes request will come to the server.

Semantic must be designed in such a way that consistence state of DFS will maintain properly.

Test Your Progress

1. What are the design issues of DFS?
2. What do you mean by naming and name resolution?
3. Explain cache consistency approach.

7.4 Mechanism for Building Distributed File System

7.4.1 Mounting

This mechanism is represented by a hierarchically structured system. It is UNIX specific. A filename space can be bounded to or mounted at an internal node or a leaf node of a namespace tree. A node onto which a namespace is mounted is called *mount point*.

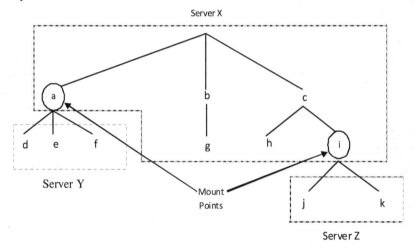

Figure 7.3: Name Space Hierarchy

In Figure 7.3 nodes **a** and **i** are mounts at which directories at stored at Server Y and Server Z are mounted. Note that **a** and **i** are internal nodes in namespace tree. The kernel maintains a mount table, which maps mount points to appropriate storage devices. Whenever a file access path crosses a mount point, this is intercepted by the kernel, which then obtains the required service from the remote server.

Uses of Mounting in DFS

To maintain the mount information, DFS is maintained by remote server, which will mount at client so that each client has information about file servers. There are two approaches to maintain mount information. Let us discuss each of them in brief.

- **Approach 1:** Clients maintain mount information in which each client has to independently mount every required file system. When files are moved to a different server then mount information must be updated in mount table of every client.

- **Approach 2:** Mount information is maintained at servers. If files are moved to different servers, then mount information need only be updated at servers.

7.4.2 Caching

Caching is the architectural feature which contributes the most to performance in a distributed file system. Caching exploits temporal locality of reference. A copy of data stored at a remote server is brought to the client. Other metadata, such as directories, protection and file status or location information also exhibit locality of reference and are good candidates for caching. Data can be cached in main memory or on the local disk. A key issue is the size of cached units, whether entire files or individual file blocks are cached. Caching entire files is simpler and most files in fact read sequentially in their entirety, but files which are larger than the client cache cannot be fetched. Cache validation can be done in two ways. The client can contact the server before accessing the cache or the server can notify clients when data is rendered stale. This can reduce client/server traffic. A number of approaches to propagating changes back to the server are also possible. A change may be propagated when the file is closed or by deferring it for a set period of time. This would be useful where files are overwritten frequently. A policy of deferred update is also useful in situations where a host can become disconnected from the network and propagates updates upon reconnection.

7.4. Hints

Caching is an important mechanism to improve the performance of a file system, however, guaranteeing the consistency of the cached items requires elaborate and expensive client/server protocols. An alternative approach to maintaining consistency is to treat cached data (mostly Metadata) as _hints_. With this scheme, cached data is not expected to be completely consistent, but when it is, it can dramatically improve performance. For maximum performance benefit, a hint should nearly always be correct. To prevent the occurrence of negative consequences if a hint is erroneous, the classes of applications that use hints must be restricted to those that can recover after discovering that the cached data is invalid, that is, the data should be self-validating upon use. Note that file data cannot be treated as a hint because use of the cached copy will not reveal whether it is current or stale. For example, after the name of a file or directory is mapped to a physical object in the server, the address of that object can be stored as a hint in the client's cache. If the address fails to map to the object on a subsequent access, it is purged from the cache and the client must consult with the file server to determine the actual location of the object. It is unlikely that file locations will change frequently over time and so use of hints can benefit access performance.

7.4.4 Bulk Data Transfer

In this mechanism, multiple consecutive data blocks are transferred from server to client. This reduces file access overhead by obtaining multiple numbers of blocks with a single seek, by formatting and transmitting multiple numbers of large packets in single context switch and by reducing the number of acknowledgement that need to be sent. For small amount of data, the transit time across the network is low, but there are relatively high latency costs involved with the communication protocols establishing peer connections, packaging the small data packets for individual transmission and acknowledging receipt of each packet at each layer. Bulk transfer amortizes the cost of the fixed communication protocol overheads and possibly disk seek time over many consecutive blocks of a file. Bulk transfer protocols depend on the spatial locality of reference within files for effectiveness. Remember there is substantial empirical evidence that files are read in their entirety. File server performance may be enhanced by transmitting a number of consecutive file blocks in response to a client block request.

7.4.5 Encryption

Encryption is used for enforcing security in distributed systems. A number of possible threats exist, such as unauthorized release of information, unauthorized modification of information, or unauthorized denial of resources. Encryption prevents unauthorized release and modification of information.

The Kerberos protocol is most commonly used mechanism which employs encryption for establishing trusted communication between two parties and for generating a private session key for initially encrypting and decrypting subsequent messages between them. Private session keys tend to be shorter than those used for public key encryption and this makes it cheaper (easier) to perform the encryption.

For performance, encryption/decryption may be performed by special hardware at the client and server. It may be difficult to justify the cost or need for this hardware to users. The benefit is not as tangible as extra memory, processor speed or graphics capability and may be viewed as an expensive frill until the importance of security is perceived.

Test Your Progress

1. Explain mechanisms for building distributed file system.
2. What do you mean by bulk data transfer?
3. What do you mean by caching and how it is useful in DFS?

7.5 Log-Structured File System

A log-structure file system maintains all updates to disk in a sequential manner like a log structure, it will speed up the process of both crash recovery and file writing. It maintains a data in indexing manner so that file can be read or written back using log efficiently. We divide the logs into segments and use a segment cleaner to compress the live information from heavily fragmented segments.

7.5.1 Disk Space Management:

In order to work for a log-structured file system efficiently, large extents of free disk space must always be available to write new data. Free disk space typically becomes fragmented over time, as files are deleted or overwritten. There are two choices for reclaiming the free space: Threading and Copying. In threading, live data is left in its place and the log is spread across free space. In this approach disk space eventually becomes severely fragmented, and this requires many disk seeks to write a log. Thus, the threading performance of a log-structured file system is no faster than traditional file system.

In the copying technique, live data is copied out of logs into a compact form thus it frees up large extents of contiguous disk space as shown in Figure 7.4. The major disadvantage of this approach is the cost of copying. Note that long-lived files can be copied over and over again. Other questions that need to be addressed are: when should copying be done, how much disk space should be free up at a time, and which blocks are selected for copying data out.

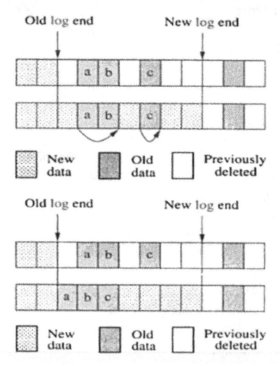

Figure 7.4: Copy and Compact Log

And a sprite log-structured file system uses a technique that use copying and threading both processes. In this technique disk space is divided into large segments, such that reading and writing a segment is much more expansive than a seek to the beginning of a segment. Logs are threaded through segments. Segments are written continuously from the beginning to the end, and before a segment can be rewritten, all the live data must be copied out of the segment.

Test Your Progress

1. What is log-structured file system?
2. Explain disk space management.

7.6 Summary

Distributed file system is file system that allows access to files from multiple hosts sharing via a computer network. This makes it possible for multiple users on multiple machines to share files and storage resources.

7.7 Key Terms

- **Cache manager:** A process that implements caching.
- **Encryption:** The process of encoding messages or information in such a way that only authorized persons can read it.
- **Mount point:** A node onto which a namespace is mounted.
- **Name resolution:** The process of mapping a name to an object or multiple objects.
- **Semantic**: The field concerned with the rigorous mathematical study of the meaning of programming languages.
- **Volumes:** Group of files.

7.8 Exercise

1. Explain the requirement of distributed file system.
2. What is difference between access transparency and structure transparency?
3. Explain various design issues of file system.
4. What are the goals of distributed file system? Write about the requirements?
5. What do you understand by DFS in distributed system? Discuss the architecture of DFS.
6. Explain caching and mounting process.
7. Name the main components of DFS.

Chapter 8
Distributed Shared Memory

8.1   Introduction

Distributed Shared Memory (DSM) is a concept of abstraction which is used for sharing of data between distributes computers that do not have shared physical memory. Distributed shared memory is known as one of the most valuable and attractive approaches for building large scale, high-performance multiprocessor system. A DSM is a mechanism which allows the end-users' processes to access data without using the inter-process communications. The goal of a distributed shared memory is to make inter-process communications transparent to the end-users. Distributed shared memory is a tool for parallel applications or for any distributed application or group of applications in which shared data items can be accessed directly. Some points about DSM are:

- DSM system provides a virtual address space which is shared among all devices present in a distributed system.

- With distributed shared memory, programs access data in shared address space is same as they access data in traditional virtual memory.

- In distributed shared memory, each device can own the data which is stored in the shared address space, the ownership can be change when data moves from one node to another.

- The distributed shared memory software layer is implemented in the kernel of the device or as a runtime library routine which maps shared memory address to the physical memory address, when a process of a node accesses data in the shared address space.

In the absence of physically shared memory message passing cannot be avoided altogether in distributed system, the distributed shared memory runtime support has to send updates in messages between computers. Distributed shared memory manages replicated data, each node has a local copy of the recently accessed data stored in distributed shared memory, for speed of access.

Advantages of Distributed Shared Memory

- Distributed shared memory systems are cheaper than tightly-coupled multiprocessor systems.

- Distributed shared memory hides the explicit message passing and provides a simpler abstraction for shared data that programmers are used to.

- Large physical memory can be formed by DSM.
- It takes advantages of the memory reference locality where data is moved in the unit of pages.
- Programs for shared memory multiprocessors can be ported to distributed shared memory.
- Shared memory gives process-to-process communication which remains transparent, and if desired, it can remove the user from any explicit awareness of communication.
- Shared memory programs are usually short in length and easy to understand than message passing programs. The memory accessing approach is already popular with users.

Challenges in DSM

- To keep track of the location of data stored in remote location.
- To overcome the high overhead and communication delays associated with the references to data stored in remote location.
- To allow concurrent accesses to shared data.

Test Your Progress

1. What do you mean by distributed shared memory?
2. What are the advantages and disadvantages of distributed shared memory?

8.2 DSM Motivation and Architecture

Motivation

- Natural transition from sequential to distributed application.
- Data locality, on-demand data movement, and larger RAMs (Random Access Memory) reduce network traffic due to remote paging.
- Better performance of some applications.
- Sender and receiver should not know each other.
- Flexible communication environment.
- Migration is completed only by transferring the corresponding PCB (Process Control Block) to the destination.
- No need to coexist the sender and receiver at the same time.
- Ease of process migration.

DSM Architecture

A memory reference can be made by any processor to any memory location which is physically separated memories that can be addressed as one logically shared address space. These types of systems are called DSM. Address space is shared in shared memory, two processors can refer to the same memory location. Memory references that can be made by any processor to any memory location, is called Non-uniform Memory Access (NUMA).

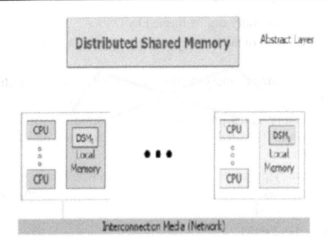

Figure 8.1: DSM Architecture

Test Your Progress

1.   Explain with diagram architecture of distributed shared memory.
2.   State the full form of NUMA.

8.3   Design Issues in Distributed Shared Memory

There are too many design issues that must be considered while designing a DSM system. An issue that is related to the structure of DSM is the granularity of sharing. Conceptually, all processes share the entire contents of a DSM. As programs sharing DSM execute, however, only certain parts of the data are actually shared and then only for certain times during the execution. It would clearly be very wasteful for the DSM implementation always to transmit the entire contents of DSM as processes access and update it. What should be the unit of sharing in a DSM implementation? That is, when a process has written to DSM, which data does the DSM runtime send in order to provide consistent values elsewhere?

8.3.1 Granularity

Granularity is concerned with the data transfer processing. Since we are building the system's virtual memory system, a restriction is associated with the data in which units of data are multiples of the node's size of the page. Larger pages are attractive over many localized accesses since the cost of migration gets amortized. A larger page also increases the chance that multiple objects will reside in that one page, known as *false sharing.* It happens when a process needs to access one memory location and some other process needs to access other memory location, non-overlapping, memory locations but both memory locations are mapped into the same page. When two computers want to access the same page, then that page will have to be constantly transferred between that two computers which leads to *thrashing*.

To avoid thrashing, it is good to allow multiple copies of shared data to reside at multiple computers simultaneously. Replication of data reduces the average cost of the read operations since simultaneous read operations can be executed locally at multiple nodes. However, writes become more expensive than reads since each cached copy of data needs to be invalidated or updated. If the ratio of read operations over write operations is sufficiently large, this might still be a worthwhile tradeoff. Similar to DFS file caching, a basic design for replication of data can be implemented, to allow only one node to have a read/write copy of a page or allow DSM multiple nodes to have read/only copies of a page, which is known as **multiple-readers single-writer replications scheme**. On a reads, the system will acquire a read only copy of the block if a block is not local. By doing this, any node that has the block of memory cached (with write permissions enabled) will downgrade to read only permissions. On writes, if the block is neither local nor no write permissions exist, the distributed shared memory will invalidate all copies of the block at other hosts and get an exclusive copy of the block. The distributed shared memory must keep track of the nodes that have a copy of the block of data. Read/write replication scheme can be extended to full replication scheme, where multiple hosts will have read/write access on shared data by using a **multiple-readers/multiple-writers**.

8.3.2 Page Replacement

A memory management scheme has to address the issues of page replacement because the physical memory is limited. In distributed shared memory which supports data movement, traditional methods like least recently used scheme, cannot be used directly in DSM. Data can be accessed in different modes which are shared, private, read only, writable, etc. To avoid degradation in the performance, a page replacement scheme would have to take the page access modes into consideration, such as private pages can be replaced before shared, as shared pages would have to be moved over the network, possibly to their owner. Read only pages can be deleted simply as their owners retains\ a copy. Thus the least recently used scheme with classes is one possible policy to handle page replacements. Once any page is selected for the replacement, distributed shared memory system must have to ensure that the page will not lost forever. One alternative is to swap the page onto disk. The page can be sent to the owner node, if the page is a replica and is not owned by the node.

Test Your Progress

1.   What are the design issues of DSM?
2.   Write short notes on:
     a.   Granularity
     b.   Page replacement concept of DSM

8.4   Algorithm for Implementing Distributed Shared Memory

Here we will discuss about four algorithms used for implementing distributed shred memory. We need to extend algorithm local address space to diverse multiple hosts connected by local area network or the Internet. Some of them can easily be integrated with distributed system.

Four basic algorithms are:

- Central server algorithm
- Migration algorithm
- Read replication algorithm
- Full replication algorithm

Let us discuss each of them in brief.

8.4.1 Central Server Algorithm

In this algorithm we will use central server, which is responsible for providing service to all clients. It provides accessing feature of shared data and maintains the shared data copy. In this approach both write and read operation take as request message from client and which will forward to data server for processor executing the operation as shown in Figure 8.2.

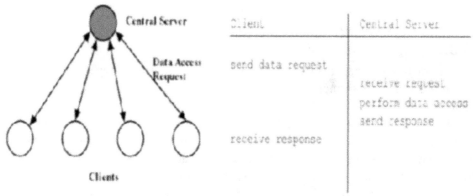

Figure 8.2: Central Server Algorithm

The data server executes the request and responds either with the data item in the case of a read operation or with an acknowledgment in the case of a write operation. It updates the data on write requests by clients and returns acknowledge messages. A simple request-response protocol can be used for communication in implementations of this algorithm. For reliability, a request is retransmitted after each timeout period with no response. This is sufficient, since the read request is idempotent; for write requests, the server must keep a sequence number for each client so that it can detect duplicate transmissions and acknowledge them appropriately. A failure condition is raised after several timeout periods with no response. Hence, this algorithm requires two messages for each data access: one from the process requesting the access to the data server and other containing the data server response. Moreover, each data access requires four packet events: two at the requesting process (one to send the request and one to receive the response) and two at the server. One potential problem with the central server is that it may become a bottleneck.

8.4.2 Migration Algorithm

In the migration algorithm, in Figure 8.3, the data is always migrated to the site where it is accessed. This is a "single reader / single writer" protocol, since only the threads processed on one host can be reading or writing a given data item at any one time. Instead of migrating individual data items, data is typically migrated between servers in a fixed size unit called a *block* to facilitate the management of the data. The advantage of this algorithm is that no message costs are incurred when a processor accesses data currently held locally.

Figure 8.3: The Migration Algorithm

If an application exhibits high locality of reference, the cost of data migration is increased over multiple accesses. However, with this algorithm, it is also possible for pages to thrash between hosts, resulting in few memory accesses between migrations and thereby poor performance. Often, the application writer will be able to control thrashing by judiciously assigning data to blocks.

A second advantage of the migration algorithm is that it can be integrated with the virtual memory system of the host operating system if the size of the block is chosen to be equal to the size of a virtual memory page (or a multiple thereof).

8.4.3 Read-Replication Algorithm

In this algorithm, only threads on one host can process data available in same block at any given time. Replicas can reduce the overhead or average cost of read operation, because this algorithm allows performing read operation simultaneously running locally at multiple hosts.

Figure 8.4: The Write Operation in the Read-Replication Algorithm.

Write operations are more expensive, because replicas must be invalidated or maintain consistency of data provided to clients or user. As per our knowledge we understand that if ratio of reads over writes is large then cost of write operation may be much more than lower average cost of read operations.

For performing any read operation on a data block that is not available locally, it is necessary to communicate remote server to first fetch a read only copy of that data block and need to change access rights to read only to any writable copy. Same as whenever need to write any data block you need to change access permission to write. This algorithm maintains the consistency of data block because always read access fetches the value of most updated write to the same location.

8.4.4 Full Replication Algorithm

Extension of read replication algorithm is known as full replication algorithm. It will allow multiple processors to have both write and read access on shared data block. Because multiple sites shared data concurrently and we need to maintain its consistency on multiple site access.

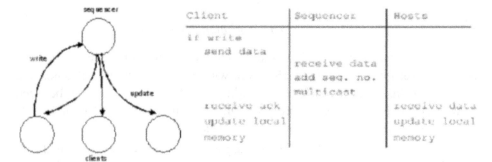

Figure 8.5: The Full-Replication Algorithm

- The multiple-readers/multiple-writers' protocol nodes have both write and read access to shared data.
- One easy way to maintain the consistency is to use a gap-free sequencer.
- All nodes wishing to modify shared data will send the modification to the sequencer. Sequencer will assign a particular sequence number and multicast the modification with the sequence number to all nodes that have a copy of the shared data item.
- Each node processes the modification requests in the sequence number order.
- At a node, there may be one or more modifications have been missed if a gap between the modification requests' sequence number and the sequence number expected.

Test Your Progress

1. What are the challenges faced in designing DSM?
2. Explain:

a. Read–Replication Algorithm

b. Full Replication Algorithm

c. Migration Algorithm

8.5 Summary

DSM is an important component of distributed system. It will enhance the functionality of distributed system. In this Chapter, we have learnt multiple algorithm to implements DSM.

8.7 Key Terms

● **Distributed shared memory**: A form of memory architecture where the (physically separate) memories can be addressed as one (logically shared) address space.

● **False sharing**: A technique in which a larger page increases the chance that multiple objects will reside in that one page.

● **Network traffic**: Data traffic is data in a network where the data is encapsulated in network packets.

● **Thrashing**: A process in which if two computers want to access the same page, then that page will have to be constantly transferred between two computers.

8.8 Exercise

1. Give an example of a distributed system. Explain why it is distributed and what advantage over a non-distributed implementation of the same system?

2. Why is it difficult to synchronize things in distributed systems?

3. Explain why it might be a problem to detect failure in a distributed system?

4. Explain, with examples, the client server model?

Practice with Ease for Examination

1. What are agreement protocols? What are agreement and validity objectives of byzantine agreement problems? (2006-07)

   Ans: See Section 6.3.1

2. What is the difference between a file service using the upload/download model and one using the remote access model? What is the difference between tree structured directory systems from a general graph structured system?

   (2006-07)

   Ans: See Section 7.3

3. Show the Byzantine agreement cannot always be reached among four processors if two processors are faulty. (2007-08)

   Ans: See Section 6.3.1

4. What are agreement protocols? What are Byzantine agreement problem, the consensus problem and Interactive consistency problem? (2008-09)

Ans: See Section 6.3.1

5. Show that the Byzantine agreement cannot always be reached among four processors if two processors are faulty.   (2011-12)

Ans: See Section 6.3.1

6. Show how a solution to the consensus problem can be used to solve the interactive consistency problem.   (2011-12)

Ans: See Section 6.3

7. In the context of Distributed File System explain following: (2011-12)

   i.   Mounting   ii.   Caching

   iii. Hints   iv.   Bulk Data Transfer

Ans: See Section 7.4

8. Explain the Read – Replication and Full – Replication algorithm for implementing Distributed Shared Memory.   (2011-12)

Ans: See Sections 8.4.3 and 8.4.4

9. What are agreement protocols? Discuss the general system model where agreement protocols are used. Give the applications of agreement protocols.

                                                                     (2011-12)

Ans: See Sections 6.1 and 6.2

10. Caching is one of the techniques used to improve access to naming data. What are the benefits of caching and what assumption must hold for it to be useful?

                                                                     (2011-12)

Ans: See Section 7.4.2

11. Describe Byzantine agreement problem, and explain its solution. Show that Byzantine agreement cannot always be reached among four processors if two processors are faulty.   (2012-13)

Ans: See Sections 6.3.1 and 6.4

12. Describe mechanisms for building distributed file system. Explain data access actions in distributed file system.   (2012-13)

Ans: See Section 7.4

13. Discuss the architecture of distributed shared memory and its advantages.

                                                                     (2012-13)

Ans: See Sections 8.1 and 8.2

14. Classify the agreement protocol. Explain the applications of agreement algorithms.   (2013-14)

Ans: See Section 6.3

15. Write and explain various issues that must be addressed in design and implementation of distributed file system.   (2013-14)

Ans: See Section 7.3

Unit–IV

Failure Recovery in Distributed Systems: Concepts in Backward and Forward recovery, Recovery in Concurrent systems, Obtaining consistent Checkpoints, Recovery in Distributed Database Systems.

Fault Tolerance: Issues in Fault Tolerance, Commit Protocols, Voting protocols, Dynamic voting protocols.

Chapter 9
Failure Recovery in Distributed System

9.1 Introduction

In computer system, to restore a system to its normal operational state is referred to as Recovery. Generally recovery is a very complicated process, but the simplest example for recovery is to restart a failed computer or to restart a failed process.

Enhanced performance and increased availability are provided by distributed systems. By executing (multiple or) many processes (which cooperate in performing a task) concurrently, enhanced performance can be checked. If any one or more than one cooperating processes fail, then the effects of the interactions of the failed processes with the other processes must be undone, or the failed processes have to be restarted from its standard operational state.

In distributed system increased availability is checked through replication (data, processes, hardware components can be replicated). If a site fails, then the copies of data that are stored on that site may miss updates. When these sites come to normal state, they become inconsistent with the rest of the system. Therefore how not to expose the system to data inconsistencies and bring back the failed site to an up-to-date state consistent with the rest of the system, is a big question for recovery in such cases.

9.2 Basic Concept

A system consists of a set of hardware and software components and it is designed to provide a specific service. The components of a system may also be the systems, having interrelationship with each other. When a system does not work in a specified manner, failure of system occurs. An erroneous state of a system is a state which leads to a system failure, by a sequence of valid state transitions.

A fault is an abnormal physical condition. The causes of a fault are design errors (such as system specification, or implementation error), manufacturing problem, damage exhaustion or other degradation, and external disturbances (such as harsh environmental conditions, electromagnetic interference, unanticipated inputs or system misuse). An error is that part of the system state which differs from its intended value.

Thus error is an expression of a fault in a system, which leads to a system failure. Therefore, to recover from a system failure, we need to rid the system state of errors. We can also say that, failure recovery is a process that involves restoring an erroneous to an error free state.

Test Your Progress

1. Define:
    i.   Error
    ii. Fault
    iii. Erroneous system state

9.3 Classification of Failures

A computer system can be classified as followed:

1. **Process Failure:** In a process failure the result of computation becomes incorrect, the state of the system deviate from specification due to process, the progress of the process may fails etc. Examples of such processes that cause error and fail to progress are deadlocks, timeouts, protection violation, wrong input by the user, consistency violation (can happen if an optimistic concurrency control technique is employed). A failed process may be aborted or restarted, this depends on the type of error that cause a process to fail.

2. **System Failure:** System failure occurs when the execution of the processor fails. This type of failure is caused by errors in software and problems in hardware (e.g. CPU (Central Processing Unit) failure, bus failure, main memory failure, power failure, etc.). When such a failure occur the system is stopped and should be restarted in a correct state. A system failure can further be classified as follows:

    (a) **Amnesia Failure:** Such type of failure occurs when a system is restarted in a predefined state and that state does not depend upon the state of the system before its failure.

    (b) **Partial–Amnesia Failure:** This type of failure occurs when a system restarts in a state wherein a part of the state is the same as the state of the system before its failure and the rest of the state is predefined, i.e., it does not depend upon the state of the system before its failure. Such type of failure occurs typically in file servers when a file server crashes and restarts, or when a system is restarted from a checkpoint.

(c) **Pause Failure:** It occurs when a system restarts in the same state it was in before the failure.

(d) **Halting Failure:** This occurs when a crashed system never restarts.

3. **Secondary Storage Failure:** This type of failure occurs when the stored data (either part of it or the entire data) cannot be accessed. Generally, such type of failures are caused by parity error, head crash, or dust particles settled on the medium. In the case of such failures, contents of secondary storage are corrupted and must be reconstructed from an archive version, and a log of activities since the archive was taken.

4. **Communication Medium Failure:** When a site cannot communicate with another operational site in the network, a communication medium failure occurs. Usually this is caused by the failure of switching nodes and/or the links of the communicating system.

Test Your Progress

1. Explain classification of failures.

2. Discuss the types of system failure.

9.4 Backward and Forward Error Recovery: An Introduction

As we know that, failure recovery is a process that restores an error–prone state to an error–free state. The two approaches for restoring an error–prone state to error–free state are:

1. Forward-Error Recovery

2. Backward-Error Recovery

Forward–Error Recovery: If the nature of errors and damages due to faults can be completely and correctly assessed, then to remove those errors in the process's (or system's) state is possible and can also enable the process (or system) to move forward. Such a technique for recovery is known as **forward-error recovery.**

Backward–Error Recovery: If the prediction of the nature of faults and to remove all the errors in the process's (or system's) state is not possible, then the process's (or system's) state can be restored to a previous error-free state of the process (or system). This technique for recovery is called **backward-error recovery**.

Backward-error recovery is simpler than forward-error recovery because it is independent of the fault and the error that are caused by the faults. Therefore, a system can recover from an arbitrary fault by restoring a process's (system's) state to a previous state. This simplification enables backward-error recovery to be provided as a general recovery mechanism to any type of process. There are some major problems associated with the backward-error recovery approach. These problems are:

- **Performance penalty**: The overhead of restoring a process (or system) state to a prior state can be pretty high.
- When processing begins from a prior state, there is no guarantee that faults will not occur again.
- Some components of the system state may not be recovered. For example, cash dispensed at an ATM (Automated Teller Machine) cannot be recovered.

On the other hand, the forward-error recovery approach incurs less overhead because in this technique only those parts of the state that deviate from the intended value need to be corrected. Therefore, this approach can be used only where the errors or damages due to faults can be correctly assessed. This is not a general technique as backward error recovery and cannot be used as a general error recovery mechanism.

Test your Progress

1. Define:
   i.   Forward Recovery
   ii.   Backward Recovery
2. List advantages and disadvantages of forward recovery.
3. List advantages and disadvantages of backward recovery.

9.5   Backward Error Recovery: A Detail Study

In this method a process is restored to a prior state hoping that the prior state is error-free state. In the execution of process, the points to which the process can later be restored are known as *recovery points*. A recovery point can be restored when the current state of a process is replaced by the state of the process at the recovery point.

In a system recovery, all of the processes that were active required to be restored to their respective recovery points and data (stored in secondary storage) improved by the process need to be restored to a proper state. To implement backward-error recovery, there are two approaches:

1. Operation-Based Approach
2. State-Based Approach

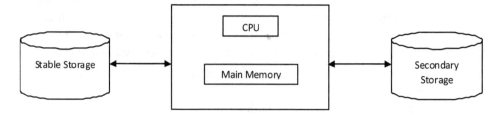

Figure 9.1: A System Model

System Model: A system consists of a single machine and is connected to a secondary storage system and stable storage system. A storage system that does not lose information in the event of system failure is known as *stable storage*. Whenever a data object (stored on the secondary storage) is accessed by a process, it is brought into the main memory if it is not there. If the access is the write operation, then the copy of the object in the main memory is updated. The data object in secondary storage is updated, when the copy of the object in the main memory is flushed to the disk by paging scheme or when the process that is updating the object terminates.

The stable storage is used for storing logs and recovery points. The contents of stable storage and secondary storage survive system failure. However, the content of stable storage are more secure than that of secondary storage.

9.5.1 Operation-Based Approach

In this approach, all the modification made to the state of a process are recorded in detail so that a previous state of the process can be restored by reversing all the changes made to the state. These record of the system activity is known as an *audit trail* or *log*.

Updating–In–Place: In this scheme, every update (write) operation to an object updates the object and results in a log to be recorded in a stable storage which has enough information to UNDO and REDO operations completely. The recorded information includes: (1) The name of the object, (2) The old state of the object (for UNDO), and (3) The new state of the object (for REDO). A recoverable update operation can be implemented as a collection of operations as follows:

- A **do** operation does the action (update) and writes a log record.
- An **UNDO** operation, (given a log record written by a **do** operation) undoes the action performed by the **do** operation.
- A **REDO** operation, (given a log record written by a **do** operation) redoes the action specified by the **do** operation.
- A **display** operation (optional), displays the log record.

The major problem in updating–in–place is that, **do** operation cannot be undone if the system crashes after an update operation but before the log record is stored. This problem is resolved by the write–ahead log protocol.

Write–Ahead–Log–Protocol: In this protocol, following two operations are used to implement a recoverable update operation:

- Update an object only after the UNDO log is recorded.
- Before committing the updates, UNDO and REDO logs are recorded.

9.5.2 State-Based Approach

In this recovery approach, the entire state of a process is saved when a recovery point is established and to recover a process involves restoring its saved state and resuming the execution of the process from the state. The state saving process is also referred as *checkpointing* or *taking a checkpoint*. The recovery points, where checkpointing occurs is referred to as *checkpoint*. The process to restore a process (system) to a prior state is referred to as **rolling back** the process.

Shadow Paging: This is a special case of state–based approach. In this approach, only a part of the system state is saved to facilitate recovery. Whenever a process need to modify an object, the page containing that object is duplicated and maintained on stable storage. After this process only one of the copies undergoes all the modifications done by the process. The other unmodified copy is known as *shadow page*. In the case of process failure, the modified copy is discarded to restore the database to a proper state. Otherwise the shadow page is discarded and modified page is made part of the database.

Test Your Progress

1.   What is backward–error recovery?
2.   Explain two approaches of backward error recovery.

9.6   Recovery in Concurrent System

Several processes cooperate by exchanging information to complete a task in concurrent systems. The exchange of information can be done through a shared memory in the case of shared memory machines (for example, multiprocessor system) or through messages in case of distributed system. In such type of systems if anyone of the cooperating processes fails and resumes its execution from a recovery point, then the effect it has caused at other processes because of exchanging information with them after establishing the recovery point, will have to be undone. To undo the effects caused by failed processes to an active process, the active process must also have to rolled back to prior state. Therefore in concurrent systems, all of the cooperating processes need to establish recovery points. To roll back processes in concurrent systems is more difficult than in the case of single process. Rolling back of processes causes further problems, which are as follows:

9.6.1 Orphan Messages and the Domino Effect

Consider Figure 9.1 shows the system activity. Here A, B, and C are three processes that cooperate by exchanging information (exchange of information is shown by arrows). The symbol '[' marks a recovery point to which a process can be rolled back in the event of a failure.

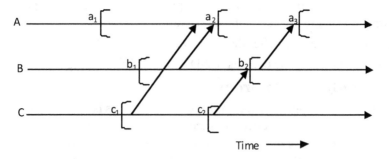

Figure 9.2: Domino Effect

If a process A needs to be rolled back, it can be roll back to the recovery point

a_3 without affecting any other process. Imagine that B fails after sending message m to A and is rolled back to b_2. In this case receipt of message m is recorded in a_3, but sending of message m from B is not recorded in b_2. Here a situation arises that A has received message m from B, but B has no record of sending it, this corresponds to an inconsistent state. Under such circumstances, m is referred as an *Orphan message* and process A after establishing its recovery point b_2. When B is rolled back to b_2, the event that is responsible for the interaction is undone. Hence, all the effect at A caused by the interaction must also be undone. This can be achieved by rolling back A to recovery point a_2. Similarly, if C is rolled back, all the three processes must roll back to their very first recovery points, i.e., a_1, b_1, and c_1. This effect where rolling back of one process causes one or more other processes to roll back, is known as the *Domino effect*.

9.6.2 Lost Messages

Suppose that check points a_1 and b_1 are chosen as the recovery points, respectively for processes A and B. In this case, the event of sending message m is recorded in a_1, while the event of receiving it at B is not recorded in b_1. If B fails after the message m, then the system is restored to state $\{a_1, b_1\}$, where message m is lost as process A has past the point where it sends message m. This condition can also arise if m is lost in the communication channel and processes A and B are in the state a_1 and b_1, respectively. Here both the conditions are indistinguishable.

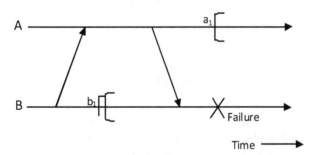

Figure 9.3: Message loss due to Roll Back Recovery

9.6.3 Problem of Livelocks

Livelock is a situation where a single failure can cause an infinite number of roll backs. Figure 9.4 shows a livelock situation in a distributed system.

Figure 9.4 (a) illustrates the activity of two processes A and B. Process B fails before receiving n_1, sent by A. When B rolled back to b_1, there is no record of sending message m_1, therefore A must be rolled back to a_1. When process B recovers it sends m_2 and receives n_1 as shown in Figure 9.4 (b). Process A after resuming from a_1, sends n_2 and receives m_2. Since A is rolled back, there is no record of sending n_1 and therefore B has to roll backed for the second time. This forces A to rollback to a_1 as it has received m_2, and there is record of sending m_2 at B. This situation can repeat infinitely, preventing the system from making any progress.

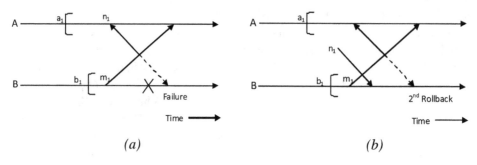

Figure 9.4: Livelock

Therefore both operation-based and state-based techniques are not suitable in locating and/or establishing usable recovery points for all the cooperating processes. There is a requirement for coordination among the processes, either at the time of establishing checkpoints or at the beginning of a recovery.

Test Your Progress

1. Explain problem of livelocks.
2. Explain orphan messages and Domino effect.

9.7   Consistent Set of Checkpoints

In distributed system, checkpointing involves taking a checkpoint by all the processes or at least by a set of processes that interact with one another while performing a distributed computation. In distributed systems, all of the sites save their *local states*, known as *local checkpoints*, and the process by which these local states are saved is called *local checkpointing*. All the local checkpoints (one from each site), collectively form a global checkpoint.

Strongly Consistent Set of Checkpoints: To overcome the Domino effect, a set of local checkpoints are needed (one for each process in a set), such that no information flow takes place between any pair of processes in the set (i.e., no orphan messages) as well as between any process in the set and any process outside the set during the interval spanned by the checkpoints. Such a set of checkpoints are referred as recovery line or strongly consistent set of checkpoints.

Consistent Set of Checkpoints: It is similar to that of a consistent global state, in that it needs that each message recorded is received in a checkpoint (state) should also be recorded as sent in another checkpoints (state).

9.8   Synchronous Checkpointing and Recovery

Koo and Toued proposed a technique for checkpointing and recovery, which takes a consistent set of checkpoints and avoids livelock problem during recovery. The algorithm's approach is said to be synchronous, because processes are involved in coordinating their local checkpointing actions such that the set of all recent checkpoints in the system is guaranteed to be consistent.

9.8.1 The Checkpointing Algorithm

For distributed system the algorithm assumes the following characteristics:

- Processes communicate by message passing through channels.
- Channels are FIFO (First In First Out) by nature.
- Failure in communication does not partition the network.

This checkpoint algorithm uses two kind of checkpointing on stable storage, i.e., **permanent** and **tentative**. A permanent checkpoint is a local checkpoint at a process and it is a part of a consistent global checkpoint. Whereas a tentative checkpoint is a temporary checkpoint which can be thought of as permanent checkpoint after successful termination of the checkpoint algorithm.

This algorithm assumes that a single process invokes the algorithm, rather than several processes concurrently invoking the algorithm to take the permanent checkpoints. The algorithm also assures that no site in the distributed system during execution of the algorithm. The algorithm has two phases:

First Phase

1. An initiating process P_i takes a tentative checkpoint and request all the processes to take tentative checkpoints.
2. Each process informs $P_{i,}$ whether it succeeded in taking tentative checkpoints or not.
3. A process say 'no' to a request if it fails to take checkpoints (due to any reason, depending upon the underlying application).
4. If P_i learns that all the processes have successfully taken tentative checkpoints, then P_i decides that all the tentative checkpoints should be made permanent otherwise P_i decides that all the tentative checkpoints should be discarded.

Second Phase

1. The initiator process P_i informs all the processes about the decision it reached at the end of the first phase.
2. After receiving message from P_i, processes will act accordingly.
3. Therefore either all or none of the processes take permanent checkpoints.

The algorithm requires that every process (once it has taken tentative checkpoint), do not send messages related to the underlying computation until it is informed of P_i's decision.

Properties: A set of permanent checkpoints taken by the algorithm is consistent because:

- Either all or none of the processes can take checkpoints.
- Set of checkpoints will be inconsistent if there is a record of a message received but not of the event sending it, which is not possible because no process sends message after taking a tentative checkpoint until the receipt of the initiating process P_i's decision, by which time all the processes would have taken checkpoints.

Optimization: As we read that the algorithm takes a consistent set of checkpoints, it may cause a process to take a checkpoint even when it is not necessary. For example, consider Figure 9.5. Let:

- $\{a_1, b_1, c_1\}$ be the consistent set of checkpoints.
- 'A' decides to initiate the checkpointing algorithm.
- It takes the tentative checkpoint a_2 and sends "take tentative checkpoint message" to processes 'B' and 'C'. Causing 'B' and 'C' to take tentative checkpoint b_2 and c_2 respectively.
- Now $\{a_2, b_2, c_2\}$ forms a consistent set of checkpoints.
- Note that $\{a_2, b_2, c_2\}$ also forms a consistent set of checkpoints. (According to checkpointing algorithm, which requires that every message recorded as "received" in a checkpoint should also be recorded as "sent" in another checkpoint and not vice-versa).

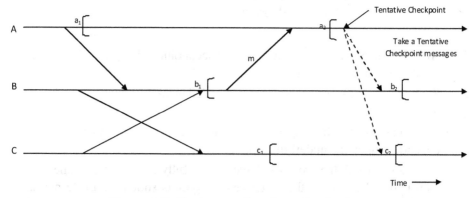

Figure 9.5: Unnecessarily taken Checkpoints

This type of unnecessary checkpointing can be avoided by using a labeling scheme discussed as follows:

- Record all messages (m) sent and received after the last checkpoint, i.e.,

    last_label_rcvd(a,b) = m.l, if m exist

    otherwise

    first_label_rcvd(a,b) = m.l, if m exist

    otherwise

- When A requests B to take a tentative checkpoint, A sends the last message received from B with its request.
- B takes a tentative checkpoint only if the last message received by A from B was sent after B sent the first message, after the last checkpoint. i.e.

    Last_label_rcvd(a,b) ≥ first_label_sent(b,a)

Therefore whenever a process takes a checkpoint, it will ask all the other processes (from which it has received message from the last checkpoint) to take checkpoints to record the sending of those messages.

9.8.2 The Rollback Recovery Algorithm

This algorithm assumes that single process invokes the algorithm as opposed to several processes concurrently invoking it to rollback and recover. This algorithm also assumes that checkpoint and rollback recovery algorithms are not concurrently invoked. The rollback recovery algothm has two phases:

First Phase

- Initiator process P_i checks whether all processes are willing to restart from their last checkpoints.

- A process may reply "no" to a restart request if it is already participating in a checkpointing or a recovery process initiated by some other process.

- If P_i informed that all the processes are willing to restart from their previous checkpoints, then P_i will decide whether all the processes should restart or they should continue with their normal activities (P_i may attempt a recovery at a later time).

Second Phase

The initiator process P_i propagates its decision to all the processes. A process will act according to Pi's decision, on receiving it.

According to the requirement of recovery algorithm, any of the process do no send messages related to the underlying computation, while it is waiting for P_i's decision.

Properties: All of the cooperating processes restart from an appropriate state because:

- All processes will either restart from their previous checkpoints or continue with their normal activities.

- If the processes have decided to be restarted, then they will resume their execution in a consistent state (as the checkpoint algorithm takes a consistent set of checkpoints).

Optimization: The recovery algorithm causes all the processes to restart from a consistent set of checkpoints, it causes all the processes to roll back irrespective of whether a process needs to roll back or not. For example consider Figure 9.6. According to the protocol, in the event of failure of process 'A', it would require processes 'A', 'B' and 'C' to be restarted from checkpoints a_2, b_2, and c_2, respectively. However there is no requirement of process 'C' to be rolled back, because there was no interaction between 'C' and the other two processes.

To minimize the number of processes to be rolled back, the rollback recovery algorithm uses the following labeling scheme:

- For any two processes A and B, let 'm' be the last message that A sent to B before A takes its latest permanent checkpoint, i.e.,

  last_label_sent (a,b) = m.l, if m exist

      otherwise

- When A requests B to restart from the permanent checkpoint, it sends last_label_sent (a,b) along with its request. But, B will restart from its permanent checkpoint only if:

  last_label_rcvd (b, a) >last_label_sent (a, b)

- This condition indicates that A is rolling back to a state where the sending of one or more messages from A to B is being undone.

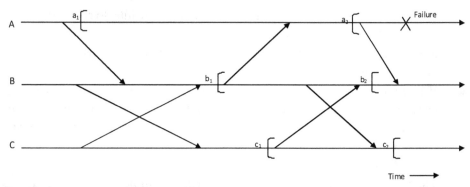

Figure 9.6: Unnecessarily Roll Back

Disadvantages of Synchronous Checkpointing

Although synchronous checkpointing simplifies recovery, it has following disadvantages also:

- Additional messages are exchanged by the checkpointing algorithm.
- During normal operations, synchronization delays are introduced.
- If failure occurs between successive checkpoints, then the synchronous approach unnecessarily burdened the system in the form of additional messages, delays and processing overhead.

Test Your Progress

1. Define local checkpoints and global checkpoints.
2. Describe synchronous checkpointing and recovery.
3. Explain checkpointing algorithm.

9.9   Asynchronous Checkpointing and Recovery

Under the asynchronous approach:

- Checkpoints at each processor are taken independently (without synchronization among processors).
- There is no surety that a set of local checkpoints taken will be a consistent set of checkpoints, before initiating recovery.
- Therefore a recovery algorithm has to search for the most recent consistent set of checkpoints, before initiating recovery.
- In Figure 9.7, the latest set of checkpoints (a_3, b_3, c_3) is not consistent and the most recent consistent set of checkpoints is (a_2, b_2, c_2).

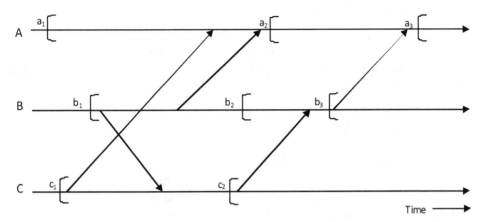

Figure 9.7: Asynchronous Checkpointing may not Result in a Consistent Set of Checkpoints

- All incoming messages are logged at each process, to minimize the amount of computation undone during a rollback.
- The messages that were received after establishing a recovery point, can be processed again in the event of a roll back to the recovery point.
- The messages received can be logged in two ways, i.e., pessimistic and optimistic.
- In pessimistic approach, an incoming message is logged before it is processed. Its drawback is that, it slows down the underlying computation, even when there is no failure.
- In optimistic approach, processors continue to perform the computation and messages received are stored in a volatile storage, which are stored in a certain intervals. In the case of system failure, an incoming message may be lost as it may not have been logged yet. Therefore in the event of rollback, the amount of computation redone during recovery is more in systems that uses optimistic logging as compared to the systems using pessimistic logging. Optimistic logging does not slow down the underlying computation during normal processing.

A Scheme for Asynchronous Checkpointing and Recovery

The algorithm proposed by Juang and Vekatesan for recovery in a system employs asynchronous checkpointing, makes the following assumption about the underlying system:

- Communication channels are reliable.
- Communication channels deliver the message in the order they were sent.
- Communication channels are assumed to have infinite buffers.
- Message transmission delay is arbitrary, but finite.
- Underlying computation is considered to be event driven, where a process P waits until a message m is received, processes the message m, changes its state, and sends zero or more messages to some of its neighbor.

Asynchronous Checkpointing

To logging in the system, two types of log storage are available, i.e., volatile and stable log. Accessing volatile log is less time consuming as compared to stable log, but the contents of volatile log can lost if the corresponding processor fails. The contents of the volatile log are flushed in a timely manner to the stable log and cleared.

Each of the processor, after an event, records a triplet (s, m, msgs, sent) in volatile storage. Here 's' is the state of the processor before the event, 'm' is the message that causes event on arrival, and 'msgs_sent' is the set of messages that were sent by the processor during the event. Therefore a local checkpoint at each processor consists of the record of an event occurring at the processor and it is taken without any synchronization with the other processors.

Notations and Data Structures

The algorithm uses the following notations and data structures:

1. $rcvd_{i \leftarrow j}$ (ckpt$_i$), represents the number of messages received by processor i from processor j, per the information stored in the checkpoint, ckpt$_i$.

2. $sent_{i \rightarrow j}$ (ckpt$_i$), represents the number of messages sent by processor i to processor j, per the information stored in the checkpoint, ckpt$_i$.

Basic Idea

- Each processor keeps track of the number of messages it has sent to the other processors as well as the number of messages it has received from the other processors.

- When a processor rolls back, it is required for all the other processors to find out whether any messages sent previously are now considered as orphan message.

- To check the existence of orphan message, compare the number of messages sent and received. If the number of received messages at a processor is greater than the number of sent messages, then there is one or more than one messages are orphan message and the process will have to be rolled back to a state where the number of messages received agrees with the number of messages sent.

- For example, consider Figure 9.8. If 'B' rolls back to a state corresponding to e_{b1}, then according to this state B has sent only one message to 'A', but according to A's state it has received two messages from B upto now. Therefore A has to roll back to a state preceding e_{a2}, to be consistent with B's state. Similarly C will also have to roll back.

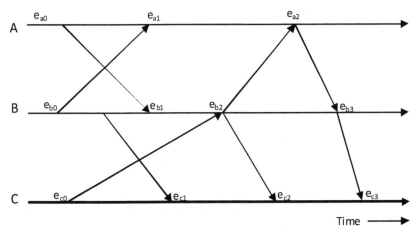

Figure 9.8: Event Driven Computation

Algorithm: The algorithm says that when a processor restarts, it will broadcast a message that it had failed. The algorithm initiates by a processor, when it restarts after failure or when it has information about another processor's failure.

At Processor i

a.   If i is a processor that is recovering after the failure, then:

    $ckpt_i$ = latest event logged in the stable storage;

else

    $ckpt_i$ = latest event that took place in i;

b.   for k = 1 to N, do   (where N is the number of processor in the system)

begin

for each neighboring processor j, do

send ROLLBACK (i, sent $_{i \to j}$ ($ckpt_i$)) message;

Wait for rollback message from every neighbor.

Note: *All the processors are executing the recovery procedure concurrently and they would have sent ROLLBACK messages to their neighbors according to step (b).*

For every ROLLBACK (j, c), message received from a neighbor j,

i does the following:

if rcvd $_{i \leftarrow j}$ ($ckpt_i$) > c, then   (which indicates the presence of orphan messages)

begin

find the latest event e such that rcvd $_{i \leftarrow j}$ (e) = c;

$ckpt_i$ = e;

end;

end;

At the end of each iteration, at least one processor will be rolled back to its final recovery point unless the current recovery points are consistent.

Test Your Progress

1. Explain asynchronous checkpoint and recovery.
2. Explain the algorithm for asynchronous checkpoint and recovery.

9.10   Checkpointing for Distributed Database System

In this section we will discuss the concepts and techniques for checkpointing and recovering in distributed systems. The two main objectives of a checkpointing algorithm for a distributed database system are as follows:

1. As we know that checkpoints are taken during the normal operation of the system, therefore it is highly desirable that normal operations should be minimally interfered by checkpointing.
2. In Distributed Database System (DDBS), all sites should take local checkpoints recording the state of the local database, because in such systems (DDBS), a process under its execution may update many different data objects at different sites.

> *Note: For fast recovery it is desired that checkpoints taken should be consistent.*

Algorithm for Checkpointing in Distributed Database System

Son and Agrawala describe the algorithm for checkpointing. Following are the assumptions made by the algorithm:

*   Transaction is the basic unit of user activity.
*   Transactions follow some of the concurrency control protocol.
*   To associate each transaction with a timestamp Lamport's logical clocks are used. (No two transactions can have same timestamp)
*   Site failure can be detected either by network protocol or by timeout mechanisms.
*   Partitioning of network never occurs.

Basic Idea: To decide the transaction, whose updates are to be included in checkpoint, all of the participating sites agree upon a special timestamp, which is known as Global Checkpoint Number (GCPN). The updates of the transactions, whose timestamps d" GCPN, are included in the checkpoint and are known as Before-Checkpoint-Transactions (BCPTs). Whereas the updates of the transactions, whose timestamp > GSPN, are not included in the checkpoint and is known as After-Checkpoint-Transaction (ACPTs).

To avoid the interference with the normal operation, when checkpointing is in progress, each site maintains multiple versions of data items in volatile storage that are being updated by ACPTs. Therefore the state of the database is not distributed once all the BCPTs terminate until the checkpointing gets complete. Whereas ACPTs continues to access the database with the help of versions.

Data Structure: The algorithm requires that each site maintains the following variables:

- **LC:** The Logical Clock (LC) maintained as per Lamport's logical clock rules.
- **LCPN (Local Checkpoint Number):** A number determined locally for the current checkpoint.

Algorithm

- A special process known as Checkpoint Coordinator (CC) initiates the algorithm.
- CC takes a consistent set of checkpoints with the help of processes known as Checkpoint-Subordinates (CS), running at every participating site.
- The CC process does not initiate checkpointing requests concurrently.

The algorithm has two phases:

First Phase

At the Checkpoint Coordinator (CC) site:

1. The CC broadcasts a Checkpoint_Request message with local timestamp LC_{cc}.
2. $LCPN_{cc} = LC_{cc}$
3. $CONVERT_{cc}$ = False
4. CC waits replies (obtaining LCPNs) from all the subordinate sites.

At all the Checkpoint Subordinates (CS) site:

1. On receipt of a Checkpoint_Request message, a site m updates its local clock. Such as:

   $$LC_m = MAX (LC_m, LC_{cc} + 1)$$

2. $LCPN_m = LC_m$
3. Site m informs $LCPN_m$ to the Checkpoint Coordinator (CC).
4. $CONVERT_m$ = False
5. Site m marks all the transactions with timestamp $> LCPN_m$ as BCPT, and marks rest of the transaction as temporary_ACPT.

After the execution of Step 5 at a site, all updates by temporary_ACPTs are stored in the buffers of the ACPTs. If a temporary_ACPT commits, then the data objects updated by it are not flushed to the database, they will be maintained as Committed Temporary Versions (CTVs). If another transaction wants to read an object for which CTV exists, then the data stored in the CTV is returned. Updates to an object that has a CTV creates another version of the object and the existing CTV is not overwritten.

Second Phase

At the Checkpoint Coordinator (CC) site

Once all the replies for the Checkpoint_Request message have been finished, the coordinator broadcasts GCPN which is decided as:

$$GCPN = Max (LCPN_1, LCPN_2, \ldots\ldots, LCPN_n,)$$

Where n is the number of sites in the system.

At all sites

1. On receiving GCPN, a site m marks all temporary ACPTs which satisfy the following condition:

    $LCPN_m$< transaction's timestamp d" GCPN

    The updates of these transactions, converted (newly) as BCPTs, are also included in the checkpoint.

2. CONVERT = True, this indicates that GCPN is known and all BCPT's have been identified.

3. When all BCPTs terminates and CONVERT = True, then site m takes a local checkpoint by saving the state of the data objects.

4. When the local checkpoint is taken, the database is updated with the committed temporary versions after which the temporary versions are deleted.

Note: *If a site m receives a new "initiate transaction" message for a new transaction whose timestamp d" $GCPN_m$ and the site m has already executed Step 1 and Step 2 of second phase, then the site m rejects the "initiate transaction" message.*

In the algorithm there is no restriction on the order in which the transaction can be executed. Due to which it is possible that the algorithm may never terminate. To ensure the termination of the algorithm a concurrency scheme, that gives priority to older transactions, is necessary. Since the number of BCPTs are finite, when checkpointing algorithm is initiated, and all of them will terminate in finite time, the checkpointing algorithm itself will terminate in finite time.

Test Your Progress

1. What are the objectives of checkpointing algorithm?
2. Explain checkpointing for distributed database system.
3. Explain the algorithm for checkpointing for distributed database system.

9.11 Recovery Replicated Distributed Database System

To improve the performance and availability, a distributed database system is replicated where the copies of data objects are stored at different sites. Such systems are known as Replicated Distributed Database System (RDDBS). In RDDBS, transaction can be continued despite of one or more site failures as long as one copy of database is available. The availability and the performance of a database system can be improved as the transactions are not blocked even when one or more site fail. Copies of the database at the failed site may miss some updates while the sites are not operational. These copies will be inconsistent with the copies at operational sites. The objective of recovery algorithm in RDDBS is to hide such inconsistencies from the user transaction, bring the copies at recovering site up-to-date with respect to the rest of the copies, and enable the recovery site to start processing transactions soon. To recover the failed sites, the following two approaches are proposed:

1. Message Spoolers: It is used to save all the updates directed toward failed sites. On recovery, the failed site processes all the missed updates before resuming the normal operations.

2. Copier Transactions: It reads the up-to-date copies at the operational sites and update the copies at the recovering sites. It runs concurrently with user transactions.

    Recovery scheme guarantees that:

1. The out-of-date replicas are not accessible to user transactions.

2. Once the out-of-date replicas are made up-to-date by using copier transaction, they are also updated along with the other copies by the user transactions.

Algorithm for Site Recovery

The recovery scheme, proposed by Bhargava and Ruan, is based on copier transaction.

System Model

The database is supposed to be manipulated through the transactions whose access to the database is controlled by concurrency control algorithm. Transactions either run to completion or they have no effect on the database. The semantics of read and write operation on the database are such that a read operation will read from any available copy and write operation update all available copies. All of the out-of-date copies in the database are assumed to be marked "unreadable". It is also assumed that database is fully replicated. A site may be in any of the following states:

1. **Operational/Up:** In this state, site is updating normal and user transactions are accepted.

2. **Recovering:** In this state, recovery is still in progress at the site and the site is not ready to accept the user transaction.

3. **Down:** In this state, no RDDBS can be performed at the site.

4. **Non-operational:** The site's state is either recovering or down.

The operational session of a site is a time period during which the site is up. Each of the operational session of a site is designated with a session number, which is unique in the site's history, but not necessarily to be unique systemwide. Session numbers are stored on a non-volatile storage so that the recovering site can use appropriate session number.

Data Structures: Each site (k) maintains the following data structure:

●   The session number of site, k, is maintained in a variable AS_k. AS_k is set to zero, when site, k, is non-operational.

● PS_k is a vector of size n (where n is the number of sites in the system). PS_k [i] is the session number of site 'i' as known to site 'k'. Since the sites are up and down dynamically, a site's knowledge of the system is not always correct. Therefore PS_k gives the state of the system as perceived by k. PS_k [i] is set to zero whenever k learns that site, i, is down or some other site informs k that site, i, is down.

We now discuss that how the system functions under normal conditions, failure and during recovery:

1. **User Transactions:** Each request that originates at a site, i, for reading or writing a data item at site, k, carries PS_i [k]. If PS_i [k] $\neq AS_k$ or $AS_k = 0$, then the request will be rejected by site, k. Otherwise, there are three possibilities: (i) The data item is reliable: the request is processed at site, k. (ii) The data item is marked unreadable and the operation is a write operation: when transaction commits, the data is modified and will be marked readable. (iii) The data item is marked unreadable and the operation is a read operation: a copier transaction is initiated by site, k.

2. **Copier Transaction:** It may be initiated for all the data items marked as unreadable, when a site starts recovering. Copier transaction, on the other hand, may be initiated on demand basis, i.e., whenever a read operation is received for individual data items, marked unreadable.

3. **Control Transaction:** These are the special transactions that update AS and PS at all sites (including any recovery site). When a recovery site (let k) decides that it is ready to change its state from recovering to operational, it initiates **type 1** control transaction; which performs the following operations:

    i.   It reads PS_i from some reachable site i and refreshes PS_k.

    ii.   It chooses a new session number, sets PS_k [k] to this new session number, writes PS_k [k] to all PS_i [k], where PS_k [i] $\neq 0$.

When site discovers that one or more sites are down, it initiates a **type 2** control transaction; which performs the following operations:

i.   It sets PS_k [m] and PS_k [n] to zero.

ii.   For all i such that PS_k [i] $\neq 0$, it sets PS_i [m] and PS_i [n] to zero.

Site Recovery Procedure

Whenever a site, k, restarts after failure, the recovery procedure at that site performs the following operations:

1. It sets $AS_k = 0$, i.e., the site, k, is recovering and is not ready to accept user transactions.

2. It marks all the copies of data items unreadable.

3. It initiates control transaction of **type 1.**

4. If Step 3 terminates successfully, then the site copies the new session number from PS_k [k] to AS_k (a new session number is set in PS_k [k] by **type 1** control transaction). When $AS_k \neq 0$, the site is ready to accept user transactions.

5.   If Step 3 fails due to failure of any other site, then site, k, initiates a **type 2**

control transaction to exclude the newly failed site and then restarts from step 3.

Recovering site will mark all the data items unreadable in Step 2. However, only those data items that missed updates while the site was non-operational need to be marked unreadable.

Test Your Progress

1. What is replication? What are its advantages and disadvantages?
2. What are the two methods used to recover from failed site?

9.12 Summary

As computers are performing day-to-day tasks as well as critical tasks, it is important that the performed work does not lost due to failures. Always it is not possible to avoid disturbances due to failures. Therefore it is very important that the work lost due to the failures should be minimum and the time taken for recovery from failure should also be minimum. In this Chapter, we have learnt about failures and failure recovery attempts

Failures are caused by errors in process state, and failure recovery attempts to remove those errors. The two approaches to remove errors from process state are (a) Backward-error recovery and (b) Forward-error recovery. Backward-error recoveries restore the process to its prior state and hope that it is error free and resumes the execution from the prior state. Whereas forward-error recovery removes the error in the process state and resumes the execution of process from that point. Generally forward-error recovery is faster.

To enable quick recovery in the case of backward-error recovery, a system saves its state (checkpoints) regularly. The two approaches to take checkpoints in concurrent systems are (a) Synchronous checkpointing and (b) Asynchronous checkpointing. In synchronous checkpointing, all the sites in the system coordinate in taking checkpoints, thus assuring that the set of checkpoints taken by them will be consistent. Therefore for recovery the system will simply restart from the consistent state stored in the checkpoint. If the failures are rare, then delays (caused due to coordination in synchronous checkpointing) can pose an unnecessary burden on the system. In asynchronous checkpointing, sites take checkpoints without communicating each other. Hence there is no surety that the set of checkpoints taken are consistent, and an attempt to restore the system to a prior state may cause Domino effect. Recovery also involves more overhead because a set of consistent checkpoints must be found before the system state can be restored to a prior state.

In transaction-oriented distributed database systems, checkpointing is complicated because the need for transactions to complete quickly and recovery to be very quick. Checkpointing is one scheme that takes consistent checkpoints, by enabling quick recovery. Whereas this scheme uses temporary versions of database objects to execute read and write operations while checkpointing is in progress, without interfering the normal operations of user transactions.

Recovery in replicated distributed database system is also complicated because of the fact that the copies at recovering sites may be inconsistent with the copies at the operational sites and the users must be protected from such inconsistencies. For the purpose of recovering site in RDDBS, outdated copies at that site can be made up-to-date by refreshing them from the other up-to-date copies by using copier transactions. At recovering site, user transactions can be either diverted to another site with up-to-date copy or provided with up-to-date data, once the outdated copy is refreshed.

9.13 Key Terms

- **ATM:** Automated Teller Machine; a cash machine.
- **Copier transaction:** Special transaction which reads the corresponding replicas at operational sites and refreshes the out-of-date copies when the data items at the recovering site are brought to up-to-date.
- **Data structure:** A logical arrangement in which data are stored for efficient search and retrieval.
- **DDBS:** Distributed Database Structure; a distributed database in which storage devices are not all attached to CPU and controlled by a distributed database management system.
- **Error:** An expression of a fault in a system.
- **Livelock:** A situation where a single failure can cause an infinite number of roll backs.
- **Shadow paging:** A technique used to achieve atomic and durable transactions, and provides the ability to manipulate pages in a database.

9.14 Exercise

1. Differentiate between fault, failure and error.
2. What do you understand by recovery in concurrent system?
3. What are the methods for implementing Backward–error recovery?
4. Discuss the problems which are caused by the rolling back of processes.
5. Write down the method for taking a consistent set of checkpoints.
6. Discuss recovery in replicated distributed database system.
7. Explain strongly consistent and consistent set of checkpoints.

Chapter 10
Fault Tolerance

10.1 Introduction

The systems are designed to be fault tolerant, for the purpose of avoiding interruption and to improve availability. The interruption of services provided to users are prevented by fault tolerant computer systems. The designing of fault tolerant computer system can be done in two ways, i.e., either a system may *mask failure* or it may exhibit *well-defined failure behavior* in the event of failure. In the case of *mask failure* designing, system continues to perform its specified function in the event of failure. Whereas, when a *well-defined failure behavior* method of designing is used, system may or may not perform the specified function in the event of failure. However, they can facilitate actions that are suitable for recovery. Redundancy is the approach used to tolerate failures. In this approach of fault tolerance, a system may consist of multiple number of processes, hardware components, copies of data, etc., with its independent failure model each. The two widely used techniques for designing a fault-tolerant system are *commit protocol*, which implement a well-defined behavior in the event of failure, and *voting protocol* which leads to mask failure in a system in the event of failure.

10.2 Issues Fault Tolerance

As it is known that a fault tolerant system must behave in a specified manner in the event of a failure. Hence, it is important to study the consequences of certain types of failures.

a.   **Process Deaths:** It is important to regain the resources that are allocated to process, when it dies, otherwise they may be permanently lost. Many of the distributed systems are structured along with the client/server model, where a client requests for a service by sending a message to a server. If the server process fails, then the client machines should be informed about the failure of a server. So that the client processes (who are waiting for reply) can be unblocked to take suitable action.

b.   **Machine Failure:** When machine fails, all the processes running at the machine will die. In the case of process death or machine or machine failure, the behavior of the client and the server processors are almost same, the only difference is that how the failure is detected. In the case when process dies, other processes including the kernel remain active. Therefore, a message with content "the process has died" can be sent to an inquiring process. An absence of any kind of message indicates either process death or a failure due to machine failure.

c. **Network Failure**: A communication link failure can partition a network into subnets, and make it impossible for a machine to communicate with another machine in a different subnet. A process cannot surely tell the difference between a machine failure and a communication link failure, except the underlying communication network (such as a slotted ring network) can distinguish a machine failure. If the communication network cannot distinguish machine failures and thus cannot return a suitable error code (such as Ethernet), a fault tolerant design will have to assume that a machine may be operating and processes on that machine are active.

Test Your Progress

1. What are the consequences of failures?
2. Write the result of a communication link failure.

10.3 Atomic Actions and Commiting

For constructing fault tolerant operation, atomic actions are the elementary building blocks. Atomic actions provide means to a system designer to specify the process interactions that are to be prevented to maintain the integrity of the system. Atomic actions have the following characteristics:

*   An action is atomic if the processes performing it are unaware of the existence of any other active process, and no other active process is aware of the activity of the processes during the time the processes are performing the action.

*   An action is atomic if the processes performing it do not communicate with other processes while the action is being performed.

*   An action is atomic if the processes performing it can detect no state change except those performed by themselves and if they do not reveal their state changes until the action is complete.

*   An action is atomic if they can be considered, so far as other processes are concerned, to be indivisible and instantaneous, such that the effects on the system are considered as if they were interleaved as opposed to concurrent.

A transaction groups a sequence of actions on a database and the group is treated as an atomic action to maintain the consistency of a database. At some point during its execution, transaction decides whether to commit or abort its actions. A *commit* is an unconditional guarantee that the transaction will be completed, even in the case of multiple failures, which implies that the effects of its actions on database will be permanent. An *abort* is an unconditional guarantee to back out of the transaction, and none of its action will persist.

To abort a transaction any of the following events can be used: deadlocks, timeouts, protection violation, wrong input provided by the user, or consistency violation. To enable backing out of an aborting transactions, the write-ahead-log protocol or shadow pages can be employed.

In distributed database system a transaction must be processed at every site or at none of the sites to maintain the integrity of the database. This is known as *global atomicity.* The protocols that enforces the global atomicity are referred to as *commit protocols.*

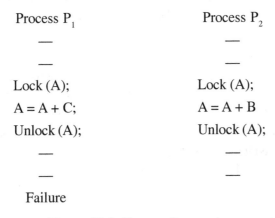

Process P_1	Process P_2
—	—
—	—
Lock (A);	Lock (A);
A = A + C;	A = A + B
Unlock (A);	Unlock (A);
—	—
—	—
Failure	

Figure 10.1: Process Interaction

Note: *Commit protocols fall into the second class of fault – tolerant design technique in that they help the system to behave in a certain way in the presence of failure.*

Test Your Progress

1. What are the characteristics of atomic actions?
2. Which protocol is employed to enable blocking out of an aborting transaction?
3. What do you mean by global atomicity?

10.4 Commit Protocols

The objective of commit protocol is to have all the sites agree either to commit or to abort a transaction. By relaxing the requirement that the number of messages employed by a commit protocol be bounded by a fixed number of messages, a commit protocol can be designed.

10.4.1 Two Phase Commit Protocol

This protocol was described by "Gray". In this protocol one of the cooperating processes acts as a *coordinator*. Other processes will be referred to as *cohort*. The protocol assumes that a stable storage is available at each site and a write–ahead log protocol is active. At the beginning of the transaction, the coordinator sends a start transaction message to every cohort.

Phase I: At the coordinator

1. The coordinator sends a *COMMIT_REQUEST* to every cohort requesting the cohorts to commit.

2.   The coordinator waits for replies from all the cohorts.

At cohorts

On receiving the *COMMIT_REQUEST* message, if the transaction executing is successful, it writes UNDO and REDO log on a stable storage and sends an *AGREE* MESSAGE to the coordinator, otherwise, it sends an *ABORT* message to the coordinator.

Phase II: At the coordinator

1.   If all cohorts reply AGREE and the coordinator also agrees, then the coordinator writes a COMMIT into the log. Then, it sends a COMMIT to all cohorts. Otherwise, it sends an ABORT message to all the cohorts.

2.   The coordinator waits for acknowledgement from each cohort.

3.   If an acknowledgement is not received from any cohort within a timeout period, the coordinator will resend the COMMIT/ABORT to that cohort.

4.   If all the acknowledgements are received, then coordinator writes a COMPLETE to the log.

At cohorts

1.   On receiving a COMMIT message, it releases all the resources and locks (held by it for executing the transaction), and sends an acknowledgement.

2.   On receiving an ABORT message, it undoes the transaction using UNDO log record, releases all the resources and locks (held by it for performing the transaction action) and sends an acknowledgement.

When there is no failure or message loss, it is easy to conclude that all sites will commit only when all the participants agree to commit. In the case of message loss, the coordinator will resend the messages after the timeout.

Site Failure

1.   If the coordinator crashes before writing COMMIT. On recovery, it broadcasts an ABORT to all the cohorts, cohorts who has agreed to commit, undo the transaction using UNDO log and abort. Other cohorts simply undo the transaction. Note that cohorts are blocked until they receive an ABORT message.

2.   If the coordinator crashes after writing COMMIT but before writing the COMPLETE record. On recovery, it broadcasts a *commit* and waits for acknowledgements. In this case also the cohorts are blocked until they receive a COMMIT j.

3.   If coordinator crashes after writing the COMPLETE, record, nothing to be done on recovery for the transactions.

4.   If a cohort crashes in Phase 1, the coordinator will abort the transaction.

5.   Suppose a cohort crashes in Phase II, i.e., after writing UNDO and REDO. On recovery, the cohort will check with the coordinator whether to ABORT/ COMMIT– Committing may require a redo operation because the cohort may have failed before updating the database.

While the two–phase commit protocol guarantees the global atomicity, it has a biggest drawback, i.e., it is a blocking protocol. Therefore, whenever the coordinator fails, cohort sits will have to wait for its recovery. In the next section we will study the non-blocking protocol, which does not block in the event of failure.

Test your Progress

1. Explain two – phase commit protocol.

10.5 Non-Blocking Commit Protocols

To make sure that commit protocols are non-blocking in the event of site failures, the operational sites should agree on the outcome of the transaction (while guaranteeing global atomicity) by examining their local states. The failed sites, on recovery, must all reach the same conclusion regarding the outcome (i.e., abort or commit) of the transaction. This decision must be consistent with final outcome at the other working sites. If the recovering sites decide the final outcome of transaction based solely on its local state, then the recovery is known as *independent recovery*.

Definitions

Synchronous Protocols: If one site never leads another site by more than one state during the execution of the protocol, then this protocol is said to be synchronous within one state transition. i.e.,

$\vee$ i, j, $t_i - t_j \leq 1$, where $1 \leq i, j \leq n$, n is the total number of sites, and t_k is the total number of state transitions that have occurred so far at site k.

Concurrency Set: Let s_i denotes the state of the site i. The set of all the states of each and every site that may be concurrent with it is concurrency set $(C(s_i))$.

Sender Set: Let s be any arbitrary state of a site, and M be the set of all messages that are received in state, s. Then the sender set for s, S(s) will be:

S(s) = {i | site i sends m and m in M}

Conditions that cause Blocking: There are some observations that lead to the conditions beneath which the two phase commit protocol blocks. Consider a case, where only one site remain operational and all the other sites fails. Now this site has to proceed solely on the basis of its local sites. Let 's' be the state of the site and C(s) contains both the commit and the abort state, then the site cannot decide whether to abort the transaction (because some other sites may be in commit state) or to commit the transaction (because some other sites may be in abort state). Therefore, the site has to block until all the failed sites recover. This observation leads to the following lemma:

Lemma: If a protocol contains a local state of a site with both abort and commit states in its concurrency set, then under independent recovery conditions it is not resilient to an arbitrary single failure.

How to Eliminate Blocking?: In Figure 10.2 only states w_i (i $\neq$ 1) have both abort and commit states in their concurrency set. For making a two-phase commit protocol a non-blocking protocol, we need to make sure that $C(w_i)$ does not contain both the abort and commit states. This can be resolved by introducing a buffer p_1 at finite state automata of Figure 10.2 (a). Buffer state at both coordinator and cohorts are introduced.

The resulting Finite State Automata (FSA) are show in Figure 10.3. Now in a system that is containing only two states: $C(w_1) = \{q_2, w_2, a_2\}$ and $C(w_2) = \{a_1, p_1, w_1\}$.

Such an extended two–phase commit protocol is non-blocking in the case of a single site failure and the failed site can perform independent recovery. Independent recovery is possible because a site can make autonomous decisions regarding the global outcome of a transaction. When a site fails, other sites can also make decisions regarding the global outcome of transaction based on their local states.

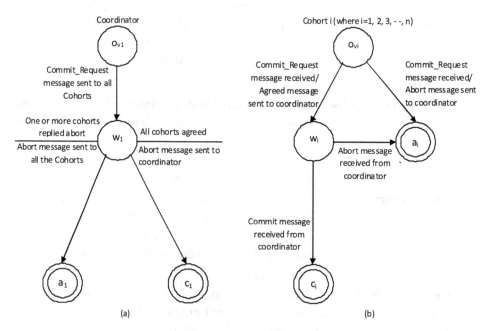

Figure 10.2: Finite State Automata Illustrating Two-Phase Commit Protocol

Failure Transitions

A *failure transition* occurs at a failed site immediately it fails or immediately after it recovers from the failure. The failure transitions are performed according to to the following rule:

- **Rule for Failure Transition:** For every non-final state, s (i.e., q_i, w_i, p_i) in the protocol, if C(s) contains a commit, then assign a failure transition from s to a commit state in its FSA. Otherwise, assign a failure transition from s to an abort state.

- **Reason:** p_i is the only state with a commit state in its concurrency set. If a site fails at pi, then it can commit on recovery. Any other state failure, safer to abort.

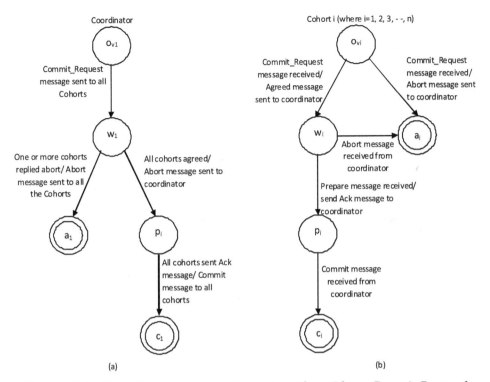

Figure 10.3: Finite State Automata Illustrating Three-Phase Commit Protocol

Timeout Transitions

If site i is waiting on a message from j (j ∈ s(i)) and site j has failed, then site i can time out. On the basis of message expected from j, we can find out that in what state j failed. Once j's state is known we can determine the state of j due to the failure transition at j. This observation leads to the timeout transition in the commit protocol at the operational sites.

Rule for Timeout Transition: For each non final state, 's' if site j is in S(s), and site j has a failure transition from s to a commit (abort) state, then assign a timeout transition from s to a commit (abort) state.

Reason: Failed site makes a transition to a commit (abort) state using failure transition rule. Therefore, the operational site must make the same transition to ensure that the final outcome of the transaction is the same at all the sites.

Non-blocking Commit Protocol

Phase 1

- The first phase of non-blocking protocol is identical to that of two-phase commit, except for failures.
- Here, coordinator is in state w_1 and each cohort is in 'a' or 'w' or 'q', depending on whether it has received the COMMIT_REQUEST message or not.

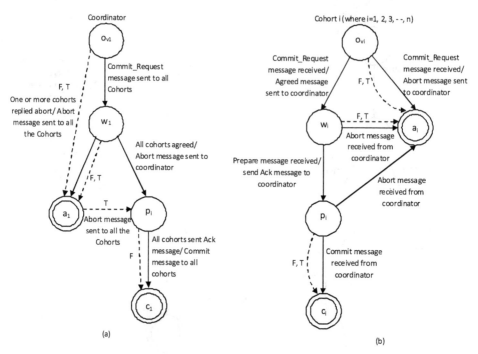

Figure 10.4: Finite State Automata Illustrating Timeout and Failure Transition

Phase 2

- A coordinator sends a Prepare message to all the cohorts (if all of them sent Agreed message in Phase 1).
- Otherwise, the coordinator will send an Abort message to them.
- After receiving a Prepare message, a cohort sends an acknowledgement to the coordinator.
  1. If the coordinator fails before sending a Prepare message, it aborts the transaction on recovery.
  2. Cohorts, on timing out on a Prepare message, also aborts the transaction.

Phase 3

- On receiving acknowledgements to Prepare messages, the coordinator sends a Commit message to all the cohorts.
- Cohort commits the transactions on receiving this message.
1. Coordinator fails before sending commit? : commits upon recovery.
2. So cohorts on Commit message timeout, commit to the transaction.
3. Cohort failed before sending an acknowledgement? : coordinator times out and sends an abort message to all others.
4. Failed cohort aborts the transaction upon recovery.
5. For example from Figure 10.4, suppose state p_i (in cohort) is not present. Let

coordinator wait in state p_1 waiting for acknowledgement. Let cohort 2 (in state w_2) acknowledge and commit. Suppose cohort 3 fails in w_3. Coordinator will time out and abort. Cohort 3 will abort on recovery., but inconsistent with Cohort 2.

Commit Protocols Disadvantages

- No protocol using the independent recovery technique for simultaneous failure of more than one site.
- The protocol is also not resilient to network partitioning.

Test Your Progress

1. Explain non-blocking commit protocol.
2. What is failure transition?
3. Discuss the process of all Phases in non-blocking commit protocol.

10.6 Voting Protocols

To replicate data at many sites is a common technique to provide fault tolerance. Commit protocols can be used to update multiple copies of data, but it cannot tolerate failures. It is necessary that sites can continue to operate even when other sites have crashed. With the voting mechanism, each replica is assigned some number of votes, and the majority of votes must be collected from a process before accessing the replica. The voting mechanism can allow access to data under network partitions, site failures, and message losses without compromising the integrity of the data.

10.6.1 Static Voting Scheme

The static voting protocol is given by **Gifford**. The basic idea behind the protocol, controls access to replicated data is as follows:

- Every replica is assigned to a certain number of votes. This number is stored on stable storage.
- A read or write operation is permitted if a certain number of votes, called *read quorum* or *write quorum*, are collected by the requesting process.

Voting Algorithm

When a process which is executing at site i, issues a read or write request for a file, the following protocol is initiated:

- Site i issues a LOCK_REQUEST to its local lock manager.
- When lock request is granted, i sends a VOTE_REQUEST message to all the sites.
- When a site j receives a VOTE_REQUEST message, it issues a LOCK_REQUEST to its lock manager. If the lock request is granted, then it returns the version number of the replica (VN_j) and the number of votes assigned to the replica (V_j) at site i.
- Site i decides whether it has the quorum or not, based on replies received within a timeout period as follows:

For read requests,

$V_r = \Sigma V_k$, $k \in P$, where P denotes the set of sites which have replied.

If $V_r \geq r$, where r is a read quorum, then site i has succeeded in obtaining the read quorum.

For write requests,

$V_w = \Sigma V_k$, $k \in Q$, where the set Q sites Q is determined as follows:

$M = \max\{VN_j : j \in P\}$

$Q = \{j \in P : VN_j = M\}$

If $V_w \geq w$, where w is the write quorum, then site i has succeeded in obtaining the write quorum.

● If i is not successful in getting the quorum, it issues a RELEASE_LOCK to the lock manager and to all sites that gave their votes. If i is successful in collecting the quorum, it checks whether its copy of file is current ($VN_i = M$). If not, it obtains the current copy. If the request is read, i reads the local copy. If write, i updates the local copy and VN. i sends all updates and VN_i to all sites in Q, i.e., update only current replicas. i sends a RELEASE_LOCK request to its lock manager as well as those in P. All sites on receiving updates, perform updates. On receiving RELEASE_LOCK, releases lock.

Vote Assignment

Let v be the total number of votes assigned to all the copies. The value of read quorum (r) and write quorum (w), are selected such that:

$r + w > v$; $w > v/2$.

The values for r and w are combined with the fact that write operations update only the current copies guarantees the following:

Above values are determined so that there is a non-null intersection between every read and write quorum, i.e., at least 1 current copy in any reading quorum gathered.

● None of the obsolete copy is updated due to write operation.

● There is a subset of replicas that are current and whose total votes is w.

● There is a non-null intersection between every read quorum and every write quorum. Therefore, in any read quorum gathered, irrespective of the sites that participate in the quorum, there will be at least one current copy which is selected for reading.

● Write quorum w is high enough to disallow simultaneous writes on two distinct subset of replicas.

● For example, in Figure 10.5, consider a system with 4 replicas at 4 sites. Votes assigned: $V_1 = 1$, $V_2 = 1$, $V_3 = 2$, and $V_4 = 1$.

Let disk latency at $S_1 = 75$ millisecond, $S_2 = 750$ millisecond, $S_3 = 750$ millisecond. And $S_4 = 100$ millisecond.

If r = 1 and w = 5, and read access time is 75 millisecond and write access is 750 millisecond.

While read operations perform well with this configurations, the inaccessibility of any one site will make the system unavailable for writes.

In Figure 10.5 let r = 3 and w = 3. The read access time is still 75 milliseconds. In addition, the system is unavailable for writes only when two sites or any three sites are inaccessible simultaneously. Therefore, by selecting the values for quorums, the configuration has been made much more reliable than the previous configuration.

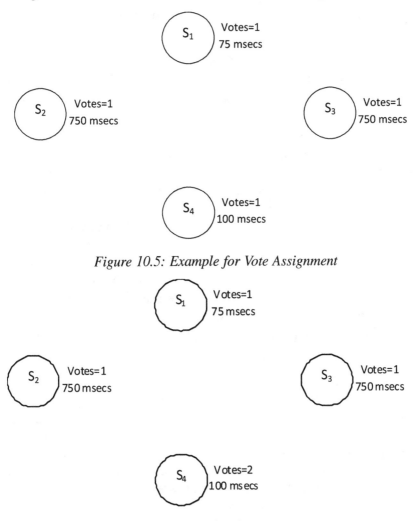

Figure 10.5: Example for Vote Assignment

Figure 10.6: Example of Vote Assignment

Consider that site 4 is known to be more reliable as compared to the other three sites. Then the voting configuration is changed (See Figure 10.6). The read quorum r = 3 and the write quorum w = 3. Now the system is unavailable for writes only when two sites (Site 4, any other site out of 3) or any three sites (excluding Site 4) are inaccessible simultaneously. As it is known that Site 4 is reliable, the system's fault tolerance is much higher as compared to the previous two configurations. Hence, the ability of a system to fault tolerance can be increased by assigning a higher number of votes to reliable sites.

The scheme is termed as *static voting* because both the criteria that decide the majority and the number of votes assigned to each of the replica remain unchanged, irrespective of the system state.

Test Your Progress

1. What do you mean by read quorum and write quorum?
2. Discuss static voting algorithm.

10.7 Dynamic Voting Protocols

This protocol provides higher availability as compared to static voting protocols, by adopting the number of votes assigned to sites or the set of sites that can form a majority to the changing state of the system.

Assume that in Figure 10.6, Site 4 becomes inaccessible from other sites due to its failure or network partition. Sites 1, 2, and 3 can still collect a quorum, however, Site 4 cannot collect quorum. If another partition or failure of site occurs (making any of the site unavailable) the system will not serve any read or write requests, because quorum cannot be collected in any partition. We can also say that the system is completely unavailable, which is a serious problem. This problem can be solved by **dynamic voting protocol,** by adapting the number of votes or the set of sites that can form a quorum, to the changing state of the system due to failure in site and communication. The two approaches to enhance availability are:

*   **Majority-based Approach:** The set of sites changes with system state. This set can form a majority to allow access to the replicated data.
*   **Dynamic-Vote Reassignment:** The number of votes assigned to a site changes dynamically.

10.8 Majority-based Approach

In this approach, the set of sites that form a majority is dynamically altered for the purpose to enhance availability in the event of site or communication failure. The set of sites that form a majority are those that were updated when the most recent update was performed. To represent the history of the network's failure and recovery, partition graph is used. In partition graph, nodes correspond to partitions and the edges represent further partitioning of the network and recovery. Two or more partitions are merged in the case of recovery.

In Figure 10.7, the root node corresponds to a system with five copies stored on five sites, which form a single partition. This specifies that all the sites are connected and all the replicas are mutually consistent. The initial single partition is fragmented into two partitions, i.e., UVX and WY. Later X is isolated from UVX and V is isolated from UV. Finally, partitions U and WY are merged to form a single partition

UWY. In the static voting protocol only UVWXY, UVX, and UWY are the partitions that allow data access, assuming that each copy has one vote.

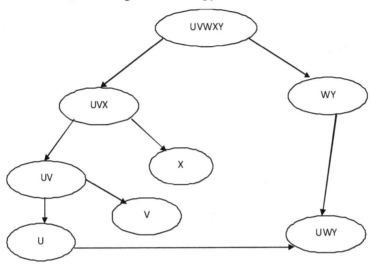

Figure 10.7: A Partition Graph

In the majority-based approach, once a system is partitioned, the protocol selects one of the partitions where read and write operations can continue. The partitioned selected is the one which could have formed a majority in the configuration that existed before the partitioning. Sites that belong to the selected partition will be able to collect quorums, whereas sites in the partitions not selected will not be able to collect quorums. According to this approach, the sites in the partitions UVWXY, UVX, UV, U, and UWY will be able to obtain quorums.

Jajodia and Mutchler proposed a majority-based dynamic voting protocol. According to this approach, each replica is stored on a distinct site and the replicas are linearly ordered a priori. The ordering is used to break ties among partitions. Each replica is associated with three variables i.e. the version number, the number of replicas updated, and the distinguished site list.

Version Number (VNi): At a site i, a version number of replica is an integer that counts the number of successful updates to the replica at i. Initially it sets to 0 and is incremented by 1 at every successful update.

Number of Replicas Updated(RU_i): It is an integer that gives the number of replicas participating in the most recent update. Initially it is equal to the total number of replicas.

Distinguished Sites List (DS_i): It is a variable at site i, that store the ID's of one or more sites. DS_i depends on RU_i.

- When RU_i is even, DS_i identifies the replica that is greater (according to linear ordering) than all the other replicas that participated in the most recent update at site i.

- When RU_i is odd, DSi is nil. Except when $RU_i = 3$ is the case when DS_i lists the three replicas that participated in the most recent update from which a majority is needed to allow access to data.

Example 10.1: Suppose there are five replicas of a file stored at sites U, V, W, X, and Y. The state of the system is shown in Table below. Each replica has been updated three times, $RU_i = 5$ for all sites. DSi is nil (as RUi is odd and ! $= 3$).

	U	V	W	X	Y
VN	3	3	3	3	3
RU	5	5	5	5	5
DS	-	-	-	-	-

Suppose V receives an update request, finds it can communicate only to sites U and W. V finds that the latest version of replicas in its partition (i.e., UVW) is version 3, and the number of replicas associated with version 3 is 5. Since partition UVW has 3 of the 5 copies, site V decides that it belongs to a distinguished partition and processes the update. As 3 sites participated in the update, therefore RU is changed to 3. Since RU = 3, then Ds lists the IDs of the three sites that participated in the update (i.e. U, V, and W). The state at this point is summarized in Table below

	U	V	W	X	Y
VN	4	4	4	3	3
RU	3	3	3	5	5
DS	UVW	UVW	UVW	-	-

Now suppose that W receives an update and finds that it can communicate only with V. It finds out that the latest version is 4 and since $RU_w = 3$, the protocol choses the static voting protocol (reason behind chosing static voting protocol isthat when the number of replicas is 3, Jojodia and Mutchler finds out that static voting is better than dynamic voting). Given that $DS_w = UVW$, V, and W form a majority among UVW and therefore W processes the update. Now the state changes to the Table below:

	U	V	W	X	Y
VN	4	5	5	3	3
RU	3	3	3	5	5
DS	UVW	UVW	UVW	-	-

Next, X makes an update and finds out that it can communicate with V,W, and Y. The latest version in VWXY is 5 with RU = 3. A majority from DS = UVW is sought and is available. Since the partition VWXY has 4 sites then RU is set to 4. As RU is even, DS set to V (which has highest lexicographical order). The current state is described in Table below:

	U	V	W	X	Y
VN	4	6	6	6	6
RU	3	4	4	4	4
DS	UVW	V	V	V	V

Consider that W receives an update, finds that it can communicate only with V. Since the partition VW has exactly half the sites in the previous partition and has the distinguished site V (DS is used to break the tie in the case of even numbers). Update can be carried out in the partition VW and the state changes as described in Table below:

	U	V	W	X	Y
VN	4	7	7	6	6
RU	3	2	2	4	4
DS	UVW	V	V	V	V

Majority-based Protocol: When site i receives an update, it executes following protocol given by Jajodia and Mutchler:

- Site, i issues a LOCK_REQUEST to its local lock manager.
- If the lock is granted, then site i issues a VOTE_REQUEST to all the sites.
- When site j receives the VOTE_REQUEST message, it issues a LOCK_REQUEST to its local lock manager. And if the lock is granted, then site j sends the values of VN_j, RU_j, and DS_j to i.
- On the basis of the responses received, site i decides whether it belongs to the distinguished partition procedure.
- If i does not belong to the distinguished partition, it issues RELEASE_LOCK to local lock manager and send Abort messages to all the other sites that responded (A site on receiving the Abort message, issues a RELEASE_LOCK request to their local lock manager).
- If i belongs to distinguished partition, it performs the update on local copy (if local copy is current). Otherwise, i obtains a current copy from one of the other sites and then performs the update (along with replica update, VN_i, RU_i, and DS_i are also updated). Site i then sends a COMMIT message to all the participating sites along with the missing updates and the values of VN_i, RU_i, and DS_i. Then it issues a RELEASE_LOCK request to local lock manager.
- When site j receives commit message, it updates its replica, and the variables VN_j, RU_j, and DS_j, and sends a RELEASE_LOCK request to local lock manager.

Distinguished Partition: When this procedure is invoked it is clear that the invoking site i has collected the responses for its VOTE_REQUEST messages. Let P denote the set of responding sites.

- Site, i calculates the values of M (the most recent version in partition), Q (set of sites containing version M), and N (the number of sites that participated in the latest update):

$$M = \max\{VN_j : j \in P\}$$
$$Q = \{j \in P : VN_j = M\}$$
$$N = RU_j, j \in Q$$

- If Cardinality (Q) > N/2, then i is a member of distinguished partition, as it has collected votes from the majority of members that participated in the latest updates.
- Cardinality (Q) = N/2, then the tie needs to be broken. Select a site $j \in Q$. If $DS_j \in Q$, then i belongs to the distinguished partition. (If N is even RU_j will also be even, and DS_j contains the highest ordered site), i.e., i is in the partition containing the distinguished site.
- Otherwise, if N = 3 and if P contains 2 or all 3 sites indicated by DS variable of the site in Q, i belongs to the distinguished partition.
- Otherwise, i does not belong to the distinguished partition.

Update: This is invoked when a site is ready to commit. The variables associated with replica at site i are updated as follows:

$$VN_i = M + 1$$
$$RU_i = Cardinality(P)$$

DS_i is updated in a following manner when $N \neq 3$ (since static voting protocol is used when N = 3).

DS_i = K if RU_i is even, where K is the highest ordered site, and
DS_i = P if RU_i = 3

Test Your Progress

1. Differentiate between static and dynamic voting algorithm.
2. Explain majority based dynamic voting algorithm.

10.9 Dynamic Vote Reassignment Protocol

In this protocol, the number of votes assigned to a site changes dynamically. "Barbara" provides the two categories of dynamic voting protocol, i.e., (i) Group consensus and (ii) Autonomous reassignment.

Group Consensus: The sites that are in active group, agrees upon the new vote assignment either by using distributed algorithm or by electing a coordinator to perform the task. Sites that are outside the active (majority) group do not receive any votes.

As this method relies on the active group's participation, therefore the current system topology will be known before deciding the vote assignments. Using this information, the method can make an intelligent vote assignment which is more resilient to future failures. Therefore to decide and to implement a vote assignment is quite complicated. A good vote assignment requires the accurate information about the current topology.

Autonomous Reassignment: The view of the system is used by each site to make a decision about changing its vote and picking a new value of vote without regard to the rest of the sites. A site in this method basically tries to obtain all or part of the votes of a sites that have been separated from the majority group. Before the changes is made final, the site must obtain approval for its vote change form a majority to ensure that the mutual exclusion provided by the voting mechanism is not compromised.

10.9.1 Autonomous Vote Reassignment

When a site selects a new value, the Autonomous Vote Reassignment (AVR) protocol is initiated. The way in which a site selects a new vote value is a policy decision.

At each site i, a vector V_i, is maintained in the stable storage, which represents the global vote assignment. $V_i[j]$, which is an element of V_i, gives the number of votes at site j according to site i. At each site i there is another vector v_i, where $v_i[j]$ represents the votes of site j as determined by site i upon the collection of votes. The V_i, and v_i are not necessarily same. Since, both the increasing and decreasing of vote values assigned to a site are allowed, it is required to keep track of currency of the vote values. This can be achieved by maintaining a version vector N at each site, $N_i[j]$ represents the version number of $V_i[j]$, at site i.

10.9.2 Vote Increasing Protocol

When a site i wishes to increase its vote value, the site performs the following steps:

1. V_i and N_i are sent by site i along with the new vote value to the sites, by which it can communicate.
2. Site i waits for the majority of the sites to respond with their votes.
3. When the majority of votes gets collected, the site i performs the following:

   $V_i[i]$ = New value, and

   $N_i[i] = N_i[i] + 1$

A site j, when receives the message sent in Step 1 and performs the following actions:

   $V_j[i]$ = New vote value of site i.

   $N_j[i] = N_i[i] + 1$

10.9.3 Vote Decreasing Protocol

Let site i wishes to decrease its vote value. Which indicates that a site is distinguishing some or all of its voting power, which does not compromise mutual exclusion. This fact profits a simple protocol where site i need not obtain majority before changing its vote value. Site i performs the following steps:

1. Set $V_i[i]$ to the new value.
2. $N_i[i] = N_i[i] + 1$.
3. Sends the vector V_i, and N_i to the other sites in the system.

A site j, when receives the above message, performs the following actions:

$$V_j[i] = V_i[i]$$
$$N_j[i] = N_i[i]$$

Vote Collecting Protocol

Suppose that site i collecting votes to decide upon the event (i.e., read, write or vote reassignment). Each of the voting site j will send V_j and N_j to site i. After receiving the responses, i follows the following steps:

1. For each reply message (V_j and N_j) received, site i takes the following actions:
   - $v_i[j] = V_j[j]$
   - If $V_j[j] > V_i[j]$ or ($V_j[j] < V_i[j]$ and $N_j[j] > N_i[j]$) then
     $V_i[j] = V_j[j]$ and $N_i[j] = N_j[j]$

   $V_j[j] > V_i[j]$ implies that site j has increased its votes since site i last determined if $V_i[j]$ and site i has to update its vector if $V_i[j]$.

   $V_j[j] < V_i[j]$ and $N_j[j] > N_i[j]$ implies that the site j has decreased its votes and the site i has to update its vector $V_i[j]$.

2. If the case arises that site i does not receive reply from site j, then it takes following actions:
   - Find out k such that $k \in G$, and $N_k[j] = \max \{N_p[j]; p \in G\}$, G is the set of all the sites from which the site i has received replies. The site k has the latest information about the votes assigned to site j.
   - $v_i[j] = V_k[j]$
     $V_i[j] = V_k[j]$
     $N_i[j] = N_k[j]$

3. Site i takes decision whether it has majority of votes or not by taking the following step:
   - Let K represents the set of all the sites in the system and G represents the sites that responded. Hence the total number of votes in the system is computed by:
     $$TOT = \Sigma \, v_i[k]; \, k \in K$$

   And the total number of votes received is computed by:
     $$RCVD = \Sigma \, v_i[k]; \, K \in G$$

   If RCVD > TOT/2, the site i has collected majority.

Test your Progress

1. Write the feature of group consensus.
2. Explain d vote reassignment protocol.

10.10 Failure Resilience

For any system to be fault–tolerant, the processes of that system must be resilient to system failures. A process may recover immediately upon recovery of the system and continue to execute from where it was interrupted due to failure. Such a process cannot be called a *resilient process* because the system may be unavailable for long duration, due to which the services provided by the process will be corrupted. A resilient process is a process that masks the failures and guarantees progress despite a certain number of system failures. The two approaches proposed to implement the resilient processes are *backup processes* and *replicated execution*

10.10.1 Backup processes

In this approach:

- Each resilient process is implemented by a primary process and one or more backup processes.
- Primary process executes while the backups are inactive.
- If primary process fails, one of the backup processes become active and take over the functions of the primary process.
- To enable this takeover and to minimize the computation, that has to be redone by backup process, the state of the primary process is checkpointed at appropriate intervals.
- Checkpointed state is stored in a place that will be available even in the case of failure of primary process.
- The advantage of backup process is that less system resources are consumed by backup processes as they are inactive.

10.10.2 Replicated execution

In this approach:

- Several processes execute the similar program concurrently.
- The computation or service continues as long as one of the process is available.
- The main advantage of replicated execution is that it provides increased reliability and availability.
- The disadvantage replicated execution is that more system resources are needed for single computation.

Test Your Progress

1. Discuss the advantage of backup process.
2. Give the two approaches for implementing resilient processes. Explain.

10.11 Reliable Communication

Let us consider a system that maintains replicated data. Assume that at each site, there is a data manager process that is responsible for maintaining the replica at that site. Suppose that a site p wishes to update a replicated data item, the following scenario may occur if p sends the update message and then fails:

- A data manager receives the update and then learns the failure of p.
- A data manager learns of the failure of p before receiving the update.
- A data manager neither receives the update nor learns of p's failure.

Under these circumstances, if a system must be fault tolerant then it is required that all the data managers behave identically. To confirm this, all the data managers are required to have an identical view of the events occurring in the system. All the data managers in the system can have an identical view if the following conditions are true:

- The messages received at them are identically ordered (helps to process messages in the similar order at all data managers).
- Each of the message is either received at every data manager or at none of them (i.e., atomic broadcast).

10.11.1 Atomic Broadcast

A communication protocol proposed by Birman and Joseph, has two phases and it is assumed that there is a queue associated with each process to store the received messages (See Figure 10.8)

First Phase

(1) The sender that wishes send a message to a group of receivers, multicasts the message to the group.

(2) The receiver on receiving the message,:

- Assigns a priority (highest among all the buffered messages' priorities) to the message, marks it as undeliverable, and buffers the message in the message queue.
- Then, it informs the sender of the priority assigned to the message.

Second Phase

1. On receiving the responses from all of the destinations, the sender:

- Chooses the highest priority assigned by all of the receivers as the final priority of the message.
- Then it sends this final priority of the message to all the receivers.

2. On receiving the final priority of a message, a receiver:

- Assigns the priority to the corresponding message.
- Marks the message as deliverable.
- Orders of the messages in the message queue-based on the increasing order of priorities.
- The message will be delivered when it reaches the head of the queue and has been marked as deliverable.

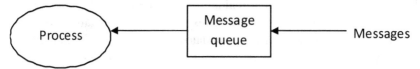

Figure 10.8: Data Structure used by Reliable Communication Protocol

If the receiver detects that it has a message marked undeliverable (whose sender has failed), then to complete the protocol it will perform the following step as a coordinator:

1. It asks all the sites regarding the status of the message. A receiver may respond in any one of the following three ways:

    - The message is marked undeliverable and the priority assigned by it to the message.

    - The message is marked deliverable and the final priority of the message.

    - It has not received the message.

2. After collecting all the responses, the coordinator will accomplish the following steps:

    - If the message was marked deliverable at any of the receivers' site, the final priority (assigned to the message) is multicasted. On the receipt of this message, receivers will perform the steps of second phase.

    - Otherwise, the coordinator reinitiates the protocol from first phase.

> **Note:** *This approach requires that even after a message is delivered by a site, it cannot be removed until all sites have received the message.*

Test Your Progress

1. Explain the reliable communication.
2. Who proposed communication protocol?

10.12 Summary

Fault tolerant computer systems can prevent the disturbance of services provided to the users. Designing of a fault–tolerant system can be done in two ways, i.e., (a) A system may mask failure (it continues to perform its specified function despite failures) (b) It may exhibit a well defined failure behavior in the event of failure (may or may not perform the specified function during failures, but it may enable actions that are suitable to recovery).

Commit protocols and voting protocols are the two widely used techniques for designing a fault tolerant system. Commit protocol implements a well-defined behavior in the event of failure, whereas voting protocol masks failure in a system in the event of failure.

Two–phase commit protocols block in the event of failure. Under independent recovery conditions, non-blocking protocols only resilient to single site failures. Voting protocols are more fault resilient than commit protocols, and can tolerate multiple site failures and communication failures as long as quorums can be obtained. Dynamic voting protocol provide high availability rather than static voting protocols by adapting the number of votes assigned to sites (or the set of sites that can form a majority to the changing state of the set).

Processes in the system should be able to endure system failures and to communicate reliably for the purpose of implementing a fault-tolerant distributed system. There are two techniques to implement processes that are resilient to system failures, i.e., (a) Backup processes stand by to take over the function of a failed process, and (b) A multiple number of processes may execute simultaneously. A system can tolerate failures, as long as one of the processes survives. A two–phase commit protocol is described as a technique to send messages reliably among processes.

10.13 Key Terms

● **Atomic broadcast:** A communication protocol proposed by Birman and Joseph.

● **Backup:** The process to the copying and archiving of computer data so it may be used to restore the original after a data loss event.

● **Lemma:** Intermediate theorem in an argument or proof.

● **Resilient process:** A process that masks the failure and guarantees progress despite a certain number of system failures.

10.14 Exercise

1. What is fault? What are the different types of fault?

2. What do you understand by fault tolerance? Discuss the issues in fault tolerance.

3. What are commit protocols?

4. What is two-phase commit protocol? Explain its operation.

5. Why one-phase atomic commit protocol is inadequate?

6. What do you understand by voting protocol? Compare and contrast static and dynamic vote protocols.

7. Explain voting assignment process with an example.

8. Discuss dynamic voting protocols.

Practice with Ease for Examination

1. Write a short note on atomic commit in distributed database system. (2009-10)
   Ans: See Section 10.3

2. What do you mean by two phase locking? How it is different from strict two phase locking? Explain. (2009-10)
   Ans: See Section 10.4.1

   Two phase locking is a process used to gain ownership of shared resources without creating the possibility for deadlock. The technique is extremely simple, and breaks up the modification of shared data into "two phases". There are three activities that take place in the "two-phase" update algorithm:

   1. Lock acquisition

   2. Modification of data

   3. Release locks

   To comply with the Strict two-phase locking protocol a transaction needs to comply with two phase locking, and release its write (exclusive) locks only after it has ended, i.e., being either committed or aborted. On the other hand, read (shared) locks are released regularly during Phase 2.

3. Explain the following: (2009-10)
   i. Fault tolerant services
   ii. Highly available services

   Ans: Fault tolerant services:

   - Improve availability/fault tolerance using replication
   - Provide service with correct behavior despite n process/server failures, as if there was only one copy of data
   - Use of replicated services
   - Operations need to be sequentially consistent when dealing with distributed read and write operation

4. With reference to the backward-error recovery explain the operation-based and state-based approach. (2010-11)

   Ans: See Sections 9.5.1 and 9.5.2

5. Non-blocking commit protocol is not resilient to multiple site failures, communication failures and network partitioning, because when a site is unreachable, the coordinator sends messages repeatedly and eventually may decide to abort the transaction. However, it is desirable that the sites continue to operate even when other sites have crashed, or at least one partition should continue to operate after the system has been partitioned. Generate an algorithm which can deal above problem. (2010-11)

   Ans: See Section 10.5 (10.5.3)

6. What do you mean by atomic commit in distributed database system? Also explain the two–phase commit protocol used for realizing atomicity in distributed system. (2010-11)

   Ans: See Sections 10.3 and 10.4.1

7. Fault tolerance can be achieved by "error processing". Describe and give examples of forward recovery, backward recovery and compensation.

   (2010-11)

   Ans: See Section 9.4

8. What is voting protocol? Compare and contrast static and dynamic vote protocols. (2010-11)

   Ans: See Sections 10.6, 10.6.1 and 10.7

9. What do you mean by failure? Give classification of failure with illustrating the examples. (2010-11)

   Ans: See Section 9.3

10. What is livelock problem in message passing system? How the synchronous checkpointing method avoids the livelock problem? Explain. (2012-13)

    Ans: See Section 9.6.3 and 9.8

11. Describe two-phase commit protocol. How the protocol handles the site failure? Write and explain its limitations.   (2012-13)

    Ans: See Section 10.4.1

12. What do you understand by dynamic voting? Explain dynamic voting protocol in brief   (2012-13)

    Ans: See Sections 10.7, 10.8, and 10.9

13. What is checkpointing in message passing system? Explain the recovery in message passing system using asynchronous checkpointing scheme.
                                                                        (2013-14)

    Ans: See Section 9.9

14. Define the livelocks. What is the difference between a deadlock and livelock?
                                                                        (2013-14)

    Ans: See Section 9.6.3

15. Show that when checkpoints are taken after every k (k>1) message sent, the recovery mechanism suffers from the Domino effect. Assume that a process takes a checkpoint immediately after sending k^{th} message but doing anything else.   (2013-14)

    Ans: See Section 9.6.1

16. Describe three–phase commit protocol. How three–phase commit protocol is different than two-phase commit protocol.   (2013-14)

    Ans: See Sections 10.4 and 10.5

Unit–V

Transactions and Concurrency Control: Transactions, Nested transactions, Locks, Optimistic Concurrency control, Timestamp ordering, Comparison of methods for concurrency control.

Distributed Transactions: Flat and nested distributed transactions, Atomic Commit protocols, Concurrency control in distributed transactions, Distributed deadlocks, Transaction recovery.

Replication: System model and group communication, Fault-tolerant services, highly available services, Transactions with replicated data.

Chapter 11
Transaction & Concurrency Control

11.1 Introduction

In this Chapter, we discuss the application of transactions and concurrency control to shared objects managed by servers. A transaction means a sequence of server operations that is guaranteed by the server to be atomic in the existence of multiple clients and server crash.

One of the main issues of this Chapter is that unless a server is carefully designed, its operations performed on behalf of different clients may sometimes interfere with one another. Such interference may result in incorrect values of the objects. We know that the use of multiple threads is beneficial to servers performance. We have also noted that the use of threads allows operations from multiple clients to run concurrently and possibly access the same objects operations that arc free from interference from concurrent operations being performed by the threads are called atomic operations.

11.2 Transactions

A transaction means a sequence of server operations that is guaranteed by the server to be atomic in the presence of multiple clients and server crashes. Transactions originate from database management system. In that context, a transaction is an execution of program that accesses a database. Transactions were introduced to distributed systems in the form of transactional file servers. We can also say transaction is an execution of a sequence of client request for file operations.

A transaction may be any read, write or compute operation on any data object of a database. The transaction process does not affect the consistent state of a database. If the database is in consistent sate before the transaction it will remain in the consistent state after the transaction occurs. It means the transaction is atomic in nature. Either, the transaction unit executes successfully or it will not execute at all. The results of a transaction are seen to the user only after the completion of the transaction.

ACID Properties: Harder and Reuter suggested the mnemonic 'ACID' which refers to the properties of transactions.

- **Atomicity:** Atomicity means that the transaction completes its processing as an unit either successfully or unsuccessfully. After the transaction. the database changes consistency or not changed at all.

- **Consistency:** Consistency means the database should be in consistent state before transaction and after the completion of transaction the database will also be in the consistent state.

- **Isolation:** Isolation means every action processed by a transaction is kept isolated until the completion of transaction, i.e., the processing is hidden from outside the transaction.

- **Durability**: Durability means any failure made after the commit operation will not affect the database. The commit action will reflect its result to its database.

To support the necessity for failure atomicity and durability the objects must be recoverable: when a server process crashes unexpectedly due to a hardware fault or a software error, the changes are reflected in permanent storage due to all completed transactions so that when the server is replaced by a new process, it can recover the objects to reflect the all-or-nothing effect. By the time a server acknowledges the completion of a client's transaction, all of the transaction's changes to the objects must have been recorded in permanent storage.

The server's aim that supports transactions is to maximize concurrency. Therefore transactions are allowed to execute concurrently if they would reflect the same effect as a serial execution, that is, they are serially equivalent or serializable.

A transaction is achieved by cooperation between a client programs. Some recoverable objects and a coordinator. The client specifies the sequence of invocations on recoverable objects that are to comprise a transaction. To achieve this, the client sends with each invocation the transaction identifier returned by open Transaction. One way to make this possible is to include an extra argument in each operation of a recoverable object to carry the TID (Transaction ID). For example, in the banking service the deposit operation might be defined:

Deposit (transaction, Amount)

Deposit amount in the account for transaction with TID transaction

Normally, a transaction completes when the client makes a close Transaction request. If the transaction has progressed normally the reply states that the transaction is committed - this constitutes an undertaking to the client that all of the changes requested in the transaction are permanently recorded and that any future transactions that access the same data will see the results of all of the changes made during the transaction.

A transaction is either successful or it is aborted in one of two ways-the client abort it or the server aborts it. Table below summarizes the list of transactions and operations performed by client and server.

Table 11.1

Successful	Aborted by client	Aborted by *server*
open Transaction	open Transaction	open Transaction
operation	operation	operation
operation	operation	operation
•	•	server aborts •
•	•	transaction -) •
operation	operation	operation ERROR
close Transaction	abort Transaction	reported to client

Figure 11.1 illustrates the transaction execution occurred in state transition diagram. The Active state occurs when the transaction starts its operation, Abort state occurs when the normal execution can no longer be performed; the Committed state occurs when the normal execution can no longer be performed, and Partially committed state occurs when the last state is reached. The Failed transactions can be restarted later either automatically or after being resubmitted by the user as new transaction as shown in Figure 11.1. (Restored to initial state)

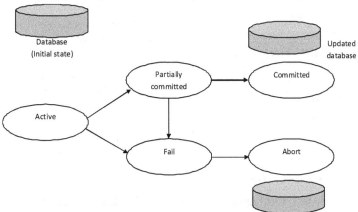

Figure 11.1: Transaction Execution: State Transition Diagram

11.2.1 Concurrency Control

We will discuss about two well-known problems of concurrent transactions: the 'lost update' problem and the 'inconsistent retrievals' problem. We also show how both of these problems can be avoided by using serially equivalent execution of transactions.

The functions we used in this section are deposit, withdraw, getBalance and setBalance. We assume throughout that each of operations is a synchronized operation, i.e., its effects on the instance variable that records the balance of an account is atomic.

The Lost Update Problem

The lost update problem comes in picture when two transactions read the old value of a variable and then use it to calculate the new value. This is illustrated as summarized in Table 11.2 by the following pair of transactions on bank accounts A, B and C whose initial balances are Rs. 100, Rs. 200 and Rs. 300, respectively. Transaction T transfers an amount from account A to B.

Transaction U transfers an amount from account C to account B. In both cases, the amount transferred is calculated to increase the balance of B by 10 percent the net effects on account B of executing the transactions T and U should be increased the balance of account B by 10 percent twice, so its final value is Rs. 242.

Now consider the effects of allowing the transactions T and U to run concurrently, as in Table 11.2. Both transactions get the balance of B as Rs. 200 and then deposit Rs. 20. The result is incorrect. Increasing the balance of account B by Rs. 20 instead of Rs. 42. This is an illustration of the 'lost update' problem. U's update is lost because T overwrites without seeing it. Both transactions have read the old value before either writes the new value.

Table 11.2: The lost update problem

Transaction T	Trainaction U
balance - b. gal:talc:mei 1:	balance b. getBalancett:
b.setBalance (balance" 1.1):	
awandraw(balance 10)	b.setBalance (balance' 1.1):
balance = b.gaBalance(i. Rs. 200	c. withdrcnribalcoice10;
	balance - b.getBa(ance0; Its. 200
b.setBalance (balance' 1.1): Rs. 220	b.saftalancetbedance *1.1): Rs. 220
b.setBalance tbalance^{1}10): Rs. 80	
	c.withdraw ebalance'10) Rs. 280

Inconsistent Retrievals

Now, we consider another example related to bank account in which transaction I transfers a sum from account A to B. and transaction W invokes the branch Total method to obtain the sum of the balances of all the accounts in the bank. The balances of the two bank accounts. A and B, are both initially Rs. 200. The result of branch Total includes the sum of A and B as Rs. 300, which is wrong. This is the illustration of the 'inconsistent retrievals' problem. W's retrievals are inconsistent because I' has performed only the withdrawal part of a transfer at the time the sum is calculated.

Table 11.3: The Inconsistent Retrievals Problem

The inconsistent retrievals problem

Transaction V		Transaction W	
a *withdraw (100)* b. *deposit (100)*		*aBranch. branch Total ti*	
withdraw (100):	**Rs. 100**		
		total = a. getBalance() *total = total + b. gethalance()* *total = total + c. getBalarsce()*	**Rs. 100** **Rs. 300**
deposit (100)	Rs. 300	• •	

Serial Equivalence

In order to eliminate such problems discussed above, if these transactions are done one at a time in some order the combined effect will also be correct. An interleaving of the operations in transactions that in which the combined effect of the operation is the same as if the transactions had been performed one operation at a time in same order is a serially equivalent interleaving.

The use of serial equivalence as criteria for correct concurrent execution prevents the occurrence of **lost updates** and **inconsistent retrievals**.

Conflicting Operations

When we say that a pair of operations confects we mean   that   their combined effect depends on the order in which they are executed. Here a pair of operations are used— read and write. Read accesses the value of an object and write changes its value. The effect of an operation refers to the value of an object set by a write operation and the result returned by a read operation.

The conflict rules for read and write operations are summarized in Table 11.4.

Table 11.4: Conflict Rules for Read and Write Operations

Operations of different transactions		Conflicts	Reason
Read	Read	No	Because the effect of a pair of read operations does not depend on the order in winch they are executed
Read	Write	Yes	Because the effect of a read and a write operation depends on the order or Their execution
Write	Write	Yes	Because the effect of a pair of write operations depends on the order of their execution.

Test Your Progress

1. What do you mean by transaction? Explain ACID property.
2. What is concurrency control? Also discuss the two problems of concurrent transaction.

11.3 Nested Transaction

In a database system, the transaction is said to be the query to the database management software program. Most often, the transaction is considered as the independent unit which produces the result of one query at once. But sometimes the result of a transaction may depend on the result of another transaction. In such case, the result is not independent.

In this manner, the transaction (query) is based on other transaction (subquery). The subquery is the part of a transaction and so called as nested transaction. These are called nested because these become the integral part of a transaction process.

The outermost transaction in a set of nested transaction is called the **top-level transaction**. Transaction other than the top-level transactions is called **subtransactions.**

Locking Rules for Nested Transaction

The aim of locking scheme for nested transaction is to serialize the object so that:

1. Each set of nested transaction is a single entity that must be prevented from observing. The partial effect on any other set of nested transaction.
2. Each transaction within a set of nested transaction must be prevented from observing the partial effect on any transaction in the set, the first rule is enforced by arranging that every lock that is acquired by a successful subtransaction is inherited by its parent when it completes.

The rules for commitment of nested transaction are following:

i. A transaction may commit or abort only after its child transactions have completed.
ii. When a sub transaction completed, it makes an independent decision either to commit provisionally or to abort.
iii. When parent abort, all of its sub transaction are aborted.
iv. When a parent sub transaction aborts the parent can decide whether to abort or not.
v. When a parent transaction commits then the entire sub transaction that have provisionally committed can commit too.

Test your Progress

1. Discuss the aim of locking scheme for nested transaction.
2. Explain locking rules for nested transaction.

11.4 Locks

In lock-based techniques, each data object has a lock associated with it A transaction can hold, request or release the lock on a data object, as required by the transaction. The transaction is said to have the locked data object, if it holds a lock. There are two modes of locking:

- **Exclusive:** If a transaction has locked the data object in exclusive lock, no other transaction can lock it in any mode. In this locking scheme, the server attempts to lock any object that is about to be used by any operation of a client transaction. If a client requests access to an object that is already locked due to another transaction, the request is suspended and the client must wait until the object is unlocked.

- **Shared:** If the transaction has locked the data object in shared mode, other transaction can concurrently lock it but only in shared mode. As we know the pairs of read operations from different transactions do not conflict, an attempt to set a read lock on an object with a read lock is always successful. All the transactions reading the same object can share their read lock.

In a locking environment, a transaction T is a sequence of various actions where various operations are performed and various data objects acted upon those actions. In addition to read and write, lock and unlock operations are also permissible actions in locking algorithm. A transaction can lock a data object with 'lock' action and can relinquish the lock by `unlock' action. A transaction is well formed if it:

- Locks a data object before accessing it.
- Does not lock a data object more than once.
- Unlocks all the data objects before it completes,
  Several locking algorithms arc listed below:
- Static locking
- Two-phase locking, etc.
  Let us discuss each of them in brief.

11.4.1 Static Locking

In static locking, a transaction acquires locks on all the data objects it needs before executing any action on the data objects. Static locking requires a transaction to predeclare all the data objects it needs for execution. A transaction unlocks all the locked data objects only after it has executed all of its actions.

Advantages

- Static locking is conceptually very simple.
- Static locking is easy to implement.

Disadvantages

- It limits concurrency, because any two transactions that have a conflict must execute serially. This may significantly limit the performance of the underlying database system.

- Another drawback of static locking is that it requires prior knowledge of the data objects to be accessed by transactions. This may be impractical in applications where the next data object to be locked depends upon the value of another data object

11.4.2 Two-Phase Locking (2PL) Protocol   (UPTU 2010)

This locking scheme is also called as 2 PL. Two-phase locking is a dynamic locking scheme in which a transaction requests a lock on a data object when it needs the data object. However, database consistency is not guaranteed if a transaction unlocks a locked data item immediately after it is done with it.

Two-phase locking is called two-phase as it has two phases:

- **Growing phase:** If is a phase during which new locks are acquired.
- **Shrinking phase:** It is a phase during which locks are released.

Two-phase locking imposes a constraint on lock acquisition and the lock release actions of a transaction to guarantee consistency. In two-phase locking a transaction cannot request a lock on any data object after it has unlocked a data object. Thus, a transaction must have acquired locks on all the needed data objects before unlocking a data object. The state of a transaction releases locks and holds locks on all the needed data objects is referred to as *lock point*.

Advantages

- It maintains database consistency.
- It increases concurrency over static locking as locks are held for shorter period.

Disadvantages

- Deadlock
- Cascade Aborts/Rollback

    Let us discuss each of the terminologies in brief.

(a) **Deadlocks:** Two phase locking is prone to deadlocks because the transaction can request a lock nn a data object while holding locks on other data objects. A set of transactions are deadlocked if they are involved in circular wait

(b) **Cascaded Abort/Rollback**: When a transaction is rolled back due to deadlock or system crashes, all the data objects modified by it are restored to their original states. In this case all the transaction that have read/write operation performed must also is restored to its previous state. This phenomenon is called *cascade rollback due to abort*. Two-phase locking suffers from this problem as the transactions may be rolled back after it has released the locks on some data objects and other transactions have read those modified.

Test Your Progress

1. Give advantages and disadvantages of static locking.
2. Explain two–phase locking protocol.

11.5 Optimistic Concurrency Control

In order to avoid the major drawbacks of locking scheme, the alternative approach is proposed by Kung and Robinson as optimistic concurrency control. Optimistic concurrency control states that the conflicts among the transaction are rare in distributed database system. It is only an assumption so called optimistic.

In optimistic concurrency control scheme, each transaction goes through three phases:

- Working phase
- Validation phase
- Update phase.

i.   **Working Phase**: During this phase, each transaction has a tentative version of each of the objects that it updates. The use of tentative versions allows the transaction to abort either during the working phase or other validation phase. The rules for read/write are:

- Read operation is performed, if the tentative version for that transaction already exists.

- Write operation records the new values of several concurrent transaction objects as tentative values which are invisible to other transactions.

ii. **Validation Phase**: When the close transaction request is received, the transaction is validated to establish whether or not its operations on objects conflicts with operations of other transaction on same objects.

iii. **Update Phase:** If the transaction is validated. All the changes recorded in its tentative versions are made permanent. Read only transaction can commit immediately alter passing validation.

Table 11.5: Validation Rules of Transactions

T1	T2	Rules
write	Read	1. T2 must not read objects written by T1
Read	write	2. T1 must not read objects written by T2
write	write	3. T2 must not write objects written by T1 and T1 must not write objects written by T2.

The Validation of a transaction must ensure that the Rules 1 and 2 are obeyed by testing for overlaps between the objects of pairs of transaction T1 and T2 as summarized in Table 11.5. There are two forms of validation - backward and forward.

Backward validation checks the transaction undergoing validation with other preceding overlapping transactions, those that entered the validation phase before it.

Forward validation checks the transaction undergoing validation with other later transactions, which are still active.

11.5.1 Backward Validation Algorithm

Backward validation: Let *start Tn* be the biggest transaction number assigned (to some other committed transaction) at the time when transaction T1 started its working phase and *finish Tn* be the biggest transaction number assigned at the time when T1 entered the validation phase. The following program describes the algorithm for the Validation of T1:

```
boolean valid = true;
for (intTi = start Tn+1; Ti< = finish Tn; Ti++) {
    if (read set of T1 intersects write set of Ti) valid =
    false;
}
```

In backward validation, the read set of the transaction being validated is compared with the write sets of other transactions that have already committed. Therefore, the only way to resolve any conflicts is to abort the transaction that is undergoing validation.

In backward validation, transactions that have no read operations (only write operations) need not be checked.

Optimistic concurrency control with backward validation requires that the write sets of old committed versions of objects corresponding to recently committed transactions arc retained until there are no invalidated overlapping transactions with which they might conflict. Whenever a transaction is successfully validated, its transaction number, start Tn and write sets are recorded in a preceding transactions list that is maintained by the transaction service. Note that this list is ordered transaction number.

11.5.2 Forward Validation Algorithm

Forward validation: In forward validation of the transaction T1. The write set of T1 is compared with the read sets of all overlapping active transactions those that are in still in their working phase (Rule 1). Rule 2 is automatically fulfilled because the active transactions do not write until after T1 has completed. Let active transactions have (consecutive) transaction identifiers $active_1$ to $active_N$, and then the following program describes the algorithm for the forward validation of T1:

```
boolean valid = true;
for (intTid = active₁; Tid< = active N; Tid ++){
    if( write set of T1 intersects read set of Tid) valid
    = false;
}
```

11.5.3 Comparison of Backward and Forward Validation

Forward validation allows flexibility in the resolution of conflicts, whereas backward validation allows only one choice - to abort the transaction being validated. In general, the read sets of transactions are much larger than the write sets. Therefore backward validation compares a possibly large read set against the old write sets, whereas forward validation checks a small write set against the read sets of active transactions. We see that backward validation has the overhead of storing old write sets until they are not longer needs. On the other hand, forward validation has to allow for new transactions starting during the validation process.

Test Your Progress

1. Explain optimistic concurrency control.
2. Write algorithms of backward validation and forward validation.
3. Compare forward and backward validation.

11.6 Timestamp Ordering

In concurrency control method based on timestamp ordering, each operation in a transaction must be validated before it is carried out. The transaction is aborted immediately, if the operation cannot be validated and can then be restarted by the client. Each transaction is assigned a unique timestamp value when it starts. The timestamp used for its position in the time sequence of transactions. Requests from transactions can be totally ordered according to their timestamps. The basic timestamp ordering rule is based on operation conflicts and is very simple as described below.

A transaction's request to write of an object is valid if and only if that object was last read and written by earlier transactions. A transaction request to read an object is valid if and only if that object was last written by an earlier transaction.

This rule assumes that there is only one version of each object and restricts access to one transaction at a time. If each transaction has its own tentative version of each object it accesses, then multiple concurrent transactions can access the same object. The timestamp ordering rule is refined to ensure that each transaction accesses a consistent set of versions of the objects. It must also ensure that the tentative versions of each object are committed in the order determined by the timestamps of the transactions that made them. This is achieved by **transactions waiting**, when necessary, for earlier transactions to complete their writes.

Test Your Progress

1. What is timestamp ordering?
2. Define the term transaction waiting.

11.7 Comparision of Methods for Concurrency Control

We have discussed three methods for controlling concurrent access to shared data:

1. Strict two-phase locking
2. Optimistic methods
3. Timestamp ordering

The timestamp ordering method is similar to two-phase locking in that both use pessimistic approaches in which conflicts between transactions are detected as each object is accessed on the one hand, timestamp ordering decides the serialization order statically when a transaction starts. On the other hand, two-phase locking decides the serialization order dynamically according to the order in which objects are accessed. Timestamp ordering and in particular multiversion timestamp ordering is better than strict two-phase locking for read only transactions. Two-phase locking is better when the operations in transactions are predominantly updates.

The pessimistic methods differ in the strategy used when a conflicting access to an object is detected. Timestamp ordering aborts the transaction immediately, whereas locking makes the transaction wait-but with a possible later penalty of aborting to avoid deadlock

When optimistic concurrency control is used, all transactions are allowed to proceed, but some are aborted when they attempt to commit, or in forward validation transactions are aborted earlier. This results in relatively efficient operation when there are few conflicts, but a substantial amount of work may have to be repeated when a transaction is aborted.

Test your Progress

1. Compare strict two-phase locking, optimistic methods, and timestamp ordering methods for concurrency control.
2. Why is optimistic concurrency control used?

11.8 Summary

You have learnt about transaction and concurrency control. The transaction and concurrency control is very much important because site or servers are at different location and it is a major issue to maintain consistency in database which will be provided to all other servers or sites.

11.9 Key Terms

● **ACID:** Atomicity, Consistency, Isolation, Durability; properties of transactions.
● **Atomic operations:** An operation performed in Java which is performed as a single unit of work without the possibility of interference from other operations.
● **Top-level transaction**: The outermost transaction in a set of nested transaction.

11.9 Exercise

1. What do mean by transaction in context of distributed system?
2. What do you mean by concurrency control in distributed transaction?
3. Why is two-phase locking used?
4. Define locking in concurrency control.
5. Describe the concept of nested transaction
6. Define strict two-phase locking.

Chapter 12
Distributed Transaction

12.1 Introduction

Distributed transaction basically refers to a term flat or nested transaction that accesses object managed by multiple servers. In this Chapter you will learn about distributed transaction.

In distributed transaction atomicity property must be maintained, so in transaction process either all of the servers involved commit the transaction or all of them abort the transaction. To achieve this, one of the servers works as a coordinator role, which will involve ensuring the same outcome at all of the servers. The manner in which the coordinator achieves this depends on the protocol chosen, a protocol known as the "two-phase commit protocol" is the most commonly used. This protocol allows the servers to communicate with one another to reach a joint decision as to whether to commit or abort.

12.2 Flat and Nested Distributed Transaction

A client transaction becomes distributed if it invokes operations several different servers. There are two different ways that distributed transactions can be structured as flat transactions and nested transactions.

In a flat transaction a client sends requests to more than one server. For example, in Figure 12.1 transaction T is a flat transaction that invokes operations on multiple objects in servers/site, X, Y and Z. A flat client transaction completes request serially, means each of its requests complete before going on to the next one. Therefore, each transaction accesses server's object sequentially, means when servers use locking then transaction can only be waiting for one object at a time.

In a nested transaction, the top-level transaction can open subtransactions and each can open further subtransactions down to any depth of nesting. Figure 12.1 shows a client's transaction T that opens two subtransactions T1 and T2, which access objects at servers X and Y. The subtransactions T1 and T2 open further subtransactions T11, T21 and T22, which access objects at servers M, N and P.

In nested transaction case, sub-transactions at the same level can run concurrently, so T1 and T2 are concurrent, and as they invoke objects in different servers, they can run in parallel. The four subtransactions T11, T12, T21 and T22 also run concurrently.

Consider a distributed transaction in which a client transfers Rs. 10 from account A to C and then transfer Rs. 20 from B to D. Accounts A and B are at separate servers X and Y and accounts C and D are at server Z. If this transaction is structured as a set of four nested transactions, as shown in Figure 12.2, the four requests (two deposit and two withdraw) can run in parallel and overall effect can be achieved with better performance than a simple transaction in which the four operations are invoked sequentially.

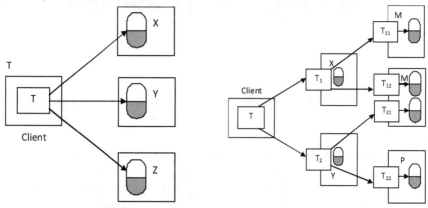

Figure 12.1: Flat and Nested Transactions

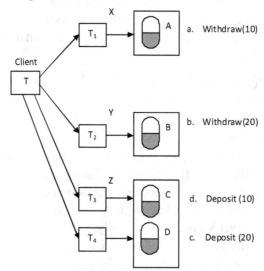

Figure 12.2: Nested Banking Transactions

12.2.1 Co-ordination in Distributed Transaction

Servers execute requests as part of a distributed transaction need to be able to communicate with one another to coordinate their actions when the transaction commits. A client can start a transaction by sending an open Transaction request to a coordinator in any server. The coordinator that is contacted carries out for the open Transaction and returns the resulting transaction identifier to the client. Transaction identifiers in distributed system must be unique. A simple way to achieve this is for a TID (Transaction ID) to contain two parts: the *server identifier* (for example, an

IP (Internet Protocol) address) of the server that initiates it and a transaction number that is a unique number to the server.

The coordinator that opens the transaction called **coordinator** for the distributed transaction and coordinator is responsible for committing or aborting transaction. Each server that manages an object accessed by a transaction becomes a **participant** in the transaction and provides an object in transaction process. Each participant is responsible for keeping track of all of the recoverable objects at that server involved in the transaction. The participants are responsible for cooperating with the coordinator in carrying out the commit protocol.

During the transaction, the coordinator maintains a list of references to the participants, and each participant records as a reference to the coordinator.

Here, interface for coordinator provides an additional method, **join**, which is used whenever a new participant joins the transaction:

Join (Trans, references to participant)

Informs to coordinator that a new arrival of participant, that has joined the transaction *Trans*.

The coordinator records the new participant in its participant list. The fact that the coordinator knows all the participants and each participant knows the coordinator will enable them to collect the information that will be needed at commit time.

Test Your Progress

1. What do you mean by distributed transaction? Also explain why it is hard to design?

2. Explain flat transaction.

3. Discuss the coordination in distributed transaction.

12.3 Atomic Commit Protocol

We know that every transaction is atomic in nature. The atomicity of transactions requires that when a distributed transaction comes to an end, either all of its operation are carried out or none of them.

Generally in distributed transaction, a client can send request for operation at more than one server. Transaction will end when client sends request that initiates a transaction, be committed or aborted. To make simple this process, coordinator communicates to all participants to asking for commit or abort current transaction? And repeat this process until coordinator receives reply from all participants. As per acknowledgement received from participants make decision for abort or commit. This is an example of a *two-phase atomic commit protocol*.

This simple one-phase atomic commit protocol is inadequate because, in the case when the client requests a commit, it does not allow a server to make a unilateral decision to abort a transaction.

In *two-phase commit protocol*, every participant is allowed to abort its part of transaction. It,is a requirement of atomicity. If any one part of transaction is aborted by its participants then coordinator will abort whole transaction.

In the *first phase of the protocol,* each participant votes for the transaction to be committed or aborted. Once a participant has voted to commit a transaction, it is not allowed to abort it. Therefore, before a participant votes to commit a transaction, it must ensure that it will eventually be able to carry *out its part of* the commit protocol, even if it fails and is replaced in the interim. A participant in a transaction is said to be in a *prepared* slate for *a transaction* if it will eventually be able to commit it. To make sure of this, each participant saves in permanent storage all of the objects that it has altered in the transaction, together with its status-prepared.

In the *second phase of the protocol*, every participant in the transaction must be carried out the joint decision. If any one of the participant votes to abort, then the decision is to be aborted the whole transaction. If all the participants vote to commit, then the decision is to commit the whole transaction.

The problem is to ensure that all of the participant vote and that they all mach the same decision. This is fairly simple if no errors occurs, but the protocol must work correctly even when some of the servers fail, messages are lost or servers are temporarily, unable to communicate with one another.

12.3.1 Two-Phase Commit Protocol

In first-phase, coordinator asks to all participants that they are prepared to commit the transaction; if they acknowledge yes, then in second-phase, coordinator tells them to commit. If any one of them acknowledged 'No', then in second phase, coordinator tells them to abort the transaction. If all participants can commit its part of a current transaction, it will agree to record the changes and maintain in permanent storage, and is prepared to commit.

The coordinator in a distributed transaction communicates with the participants to carry out the two-phase commit protocol by means of the operations summarized as follows:

Operation for two-phase commit protocol
CanCommit? (transaction)→ Yes /No

Call from coordinator to all participant to ask whether to commit a transaction.

Participant replies to coordinator with its vote in Yes/No.

DoCommit (transaction)

Call from coordinator to all participant to tell them to commit its part of a transaction.

DoAbort (transaction)

Call from coordinator to all participant to them to abort its part of a transaction.

HaveCommitted (transaction, participant)

Call from all participants to coordinator to confirm that they have committed their part of transaction.

GetDecision (transaction) →Yes/No

Call from all participants to coordinator to ask for the decision on a current transaction after they have voted **Yes** but they still had no reply after some delay used to recover from server crash or delayed messages.

Phases of Two-Phase Commit protocol

Phase 1: Voting phase

1. The coordinator sends a message CanCommit? Request to each of the participant in the current transaction.

2. When a participant receives a CanCommit? Participants replies with its vote (Yes or No) to the coordinator. Before voting Yes, a participant prepares to commit by saving objects in permanent storage. If the vote is No, then participant aborts immediately.

Phase 2: Completion according to outcome of vote

1. The coordinator receives the votes (including its own).

   (a) If there is not any failure occurs and all the votes are Yes, the coordinator makes decision to commit the transaction and sends a DoCommit request to all participants.

   (b) Otherwise the coordinator makes decision to abort the transaction and sends doAbort requests to all of them that vote 'Yes'.

2. All participants that voted 'Yes' are wait for a doCommit or doAbort request from the coordinator. When all participants receive one of these messages they will act accordingly and in the case of commit, they send a haveCommitted call as confirmation to the coordinator.

Test Your Progress

1. Explain:
   i. One-Phase Commit
   ii. Two-Phase Commit

2. Explain the performance of the two–phase commit protocol.

3. List the advantages and disadvantages of two–phase commit protocol.

12.4 Concurrency Control Indistributed Transaction

Each server manages has a set of objects and is responsible for ensuring that they remain consistent when accessed by concurrent transactions. Therefore, each server is responsible for applying concurrency control to its own objects. The members of a collection of servers of distributed transactions are jointly responsible for ensuring that they are performed in a serially equivalent manner.

12.4.1 Locking

In a distributed transaction, the locks on an object are held locally (in the same server). The local lock manager can decide whether to grant a lock or make the requesting transaction wait. However, it cannot release any locks until it knows that the transaction has been committed or aborted at all servers involved in the transaction. When locking is used for concurrency control, the objects remain locked and are unavailable for other transactions during the atomic commit protocol, although an aborted transaction releases its lock after phase one of the protocol.

As lock managers at different servers set their locks separately of one another, it may be possible that at different servers may impose different orderings of locks on transactions. Consider the interleaving of transactions T and U at servers X and Y as summarized in Table below.

T	U
Write (A) at X locks A	
	Write (B) at Y locks B
Read (B) at Y wait for U	
	Read (A) at X waits for T

The transaction T locks object A at server X and the transaction U locks object B at server T. After that, T tries to access B at server Y and waits for U's lock. Similarly transaction U tries to access A at server X and has to wait for T's lock. Therefore, we have T before U in one server and U before T in the other. These different orderings can lead to cyclic dependencies between transactions and a distributed deadlock situation arises. When deadlock is detected, a transaction is aborted to resolve the deadlock. In this case, the coordinator will be informed and will abort the transaction at the participants involved in the transaction.

12.4.2 Timestamp Ordering Concurrency Control

In a single server transaction, the coordinator issues a unique timestamp to each transaction when it starts. Serial equivalence is enforced by committing the versions of objects in the order of the timestamps of transactions that accessed them. In distributed transactions, we require that each coordinator issue globally unique timestamps. A globally unique transaction timestamp is issue to the client by the first coordinator accessed by a transaction. The transaction timestamp is passed to the coordinator at each server whose objects perform an operation in the transaction.

The servers of distributed transactions are jointly responsible for ensuring that they are performed in a serially equivalent manner. For example, if the version of an object accessed by transaction U commits after the version accessed by T at one server, then if T and U ass the same object as one another at other servers, they must commit them in the same order. To achieve the same ordering at all the servers, the coordinators must agree as to the ordering of their timestamps. A timestamp consists of a pair <local timestamp, server-id>. The agreed ordering of pairs of timestamps is based on a comparison in which the server-id part is less significant.

The same ordering of transactions can be achieved at all the servers even if their local clocks are not synchronized.

When timestamp ordering is used for concurrency control, conflicts are resolved as each operation is performed. If the resolution of a conflict requires a transaction lo be aborted, the coordinator will be informed and it will abort the transaction at all the participants. Therefore, any transaction that reaches the client request to commit should always be able to commit.

Therefore, a participant in the two-phase commit protocol will normally agree to commit. The only situation in which a participant will not agree to commit is if it had crashed during the transaction.

12.4.3 Optimistic Concurrency Control

In optimistic concurrency control, each transaction is validated before it is allowed to commit. Transaction numbers are assigned at the start of validation and transactions are serialized according to the order of the transaction numbers. A distributed transaction is validated by a collection of independent servers, each of which validates transactions that access its own objects. The validation at all of the servers takes place during the first phase of the two-phase commit protocol.

Consider the following interleaving of transactions T and U, which access objects A and B at servers X and Y, respectively.

T	U
Read (A) at X	Read (B) at Y
Write (A)	Write (B)
Read (B) at Y	Read (A) at X
Write (B)	Write (A)

The transactions access the objects in the order T before U at server X and in the order U before T at server Y. Now suppose that T and U start validation at about the same time, but server X validates T first and server Y validates U first.

In distributed optimistic transactions, each server applies a **parallel validation protocol**. This is an extension of either backward or forward validation to allow multiple transactions to be in the validation phase at the same time. If parallel validation is used, transactions will not suffer from **commitment deadlock**.

Test Your Progress

1. What do you understand by lock?
2. Define timestamp ordering rule.
3. Explain optimistic concurrency control.

12.5 Distributed Deadlocks

As we know, deadlocks can arise within a single server when locking is used for concurrency control. Servers must either present or detect and resolve deadlocks. Most deadlock detection schemes operate by finding cycles in the transaction wait-for graph.

In a distributed system invoking multiple servers being accessed by multiple transactions, a **global wait-for graph** can be constructed from the local ones. There can be a cycle in the global wait-for graph that is not in any single local one, that is, there can be a **distributed deadlock**.

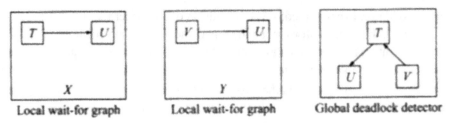

Figure 12.3: Local and Global Wait-for Graph

Detection of a distributed deadlock requires a cycle to be found in the global transaction wait-for graph that is distributed among the servers that were involved in the transactions.

A simple solution is to use centralized deadlock detection, in which one server takes on the role of global deadlock detector from time-to-time, each server sends the latest copy of its local wait-for graph to the global deadlock detector, which amalgamates the information in the local graphs in order to construct a global wait-for graph as shown in Figure 12.3. The global deadlock detector checks for cycles in the global wait-for graph. When it finds a cycle, it makes a decision on how to resolve the deadlock and informs the servers as to the transaction to be aborted to resolve the deadlock.

Centralized deadlock detection is not a good idea, because it depends on a single server to carry it out. It suffers from the usual problems associated with centralized solutions in distributed systems-poor availability, lack of fault tolerance and no ability to scale. In addition, the cost of the frequent transmission of local wait-for graphs is high. If the global graph is collected less frequently, deadlocks may take longer to be detected.

12.5.1 Edge Chasing

A distributed approach to deadlock detection uses a technique called **edge chasing** or **path pushing**. In this approach, the global wait-for graph is not constructed, but each of the servers involved has knowledge about some of its edges. The servers attempt to find cycles by forwarding message called *probes,* which follow the edges of the graph throughout the distributed system. A probe message consists of transaction wait-for relationships representing a path in the global wail-for graph.

Edge chasing algorithms have three steps: *initiation, detection* and *resolution.*

Initiation: When a server marks that a transaction T starts waiting for another transaction U, where U is waiting to access an object at another server, it initiates detection by sending a probe containing the edge < T→U> to the server of the object at which transaction U is blocked. If U is sharing a lock, probes are sent to all the holders of the lock. Sometimes further transactions may start sharing the lock later on, in which case probes can be sent to them too.

Detection: Detection consists of receiving probes and deciding whether deadlock has occurred and whether to forward the probes.

For example, when a server of an object receives a probe < T→U> (indicating that T is waiting for a transaction U that holds a local object), it checks to see whether U is also waiting for transaction. If it is, the transaction it waits for (for example, V) is added to the probe (making <T→U→ V>), and if the new transaction (V) is waiting for another object elsewhere, the probe is forwarded.

In this way, paths through the global wait-for graph are built one edge at a time. Before forwarding a probe, the server checks to see whether the transaction (for example, T) it has just added has caused the probe to contain a cycle (for example, <T→U→ V→T>). If this is the case, it has found a cycle in the graph and deadlock has been detected.

Resolution: When a cycle is detected, a transaction in the cycle is aborted to break the deadlock.

Test your Progress

1.   What are known as probes?
2.   Define:
    i.   Distributed deadlock
    ii.   Transaction priority
    iii.   Edge chasing

12.6 Transaction Recovery

The atomic property of transactions requires that the effects of all committed transactions and none of the effects of incomplete or aborted transactions are reflected in the objects they accessed. This property can be described in terms of two aspects: *Durability* and *failure atomicity.*

Durability requires that objects are saved in permanent storage and will be available indefinitely thereafter. Therefore, an acknowledgement of a client's commit request implies that all the effects of the transaction have been recorded in permanent storage as well as in the server's (volatile) objects.

Failure atomicity requires that effects of transaction are atomic even when the server crashes. Recovery is concerned with ensuring that a server's objects are durable and that the service provides failure atomicity.

Although file servers and database servers maintain data in permanent storage, other kinds of servers of recoverable objects need not do so except of recovery purposes. Here, we assume that when server is running it keeps all of its objects in its volatile memory and records its committed objects in a recovery file (files). Therefore, recovery consists of restoring the server with the latest committed versions of its objects from permanent storage.

12.6.1 Log File

In the log file technique, the recovery file represents a log containing the history of all the transactions performed by a server. It consists of values of objects, transaction status entries and intentions lists of transactions. The order of entries in the log reflects the order in which transactions have prepared.

During the normal operation of a server, its *recovery manager* is called whenever a transaction prepares to commit or aborts a transaction. When the server is prepared to commit a transaction, the recovery manager appends all the objects in its intentions list to the recovery file, followed by the current status of that transaction together with its intentions list. When a transaction is eventually committed or aborted the recovery manager appends the corresponding status of the transaction to its recovery file.

After a crash, any transaction that does not have a committed status in the log is aborted. Therefore, when a transaction commits, its committed status entry must be forced to the log, i.e., written to the log together with any other buffered entries.

Every transaction status makes entry as a pointer to the position in the recovery file. All previous transaction status entries make enable the recovery manager execute the transaction status entries in reverse order from the recovery file. The very last status entries point, in the sequence of transaction, points the checkpoint.

12.6.2 Checkpoint

A recovery manager is responsible for reorganizing its recovery file so as to make the process of recovery faster and to reduce its use of space. If the recovery file is never reorganized, then the recovery process must search backwards through the recovery file until it has found a value for each of its objects. Conceptually, the only information required for recovery is a copy of the committed versions of all the objects in the server. This would be the most compact form for the recovery file. The name **checkpointing** is used to refer to the process of writing the current committed values of a server's objects to a new recovery file, together with transaction status entries and intensions lists of transactions that have not yet been fully resolved (including information related to the two-phase commit protocol). The term checkpoint is used to refer to the information stored by the checkpointing process. The purpose of making **checkpoint** is to reduce the number of transactions to be dealt with during recovery and to reclaim file space.

12.6.3 Shadow Versions

The logging technique records transaction entries, intentions lists and objects all in the same file-the log. The shadow versions technique is an alternative way to organize a recover file. It uses a **map** to locate version of the server's objects in a file called a **version store**. The map associates the identifiers of the server's objects with the positions of their current versions in the versions store. The versions written by each transaction are shadows of previous committed versions. The transaction status entries and intentions lists are dealt with separately. Shadow versions are described first.

When a transaction is prepared to commit, any of the objects changed by the transaction are appended to the version store, leaving the corresponding committed versions unchanged. These new as yet tentative versions are called **shadow versions**.

When a transaction commits, a new map is made by copying the old map and entering the positions of the shadow versions. To complete the commit Process, the new map replaces the old map.

To restore the objects when a saver is replaced after a crash, its recovery manager reads the map and uses the information in the map to locate the objects in the version store.

Need for Transaction Status and Intentions List Entries in a Recovery File

The use of transaction status items and intentions list in the recovery file is essential for a server that is intended to participate in distributed transactions. This approach can also be useful for servers of non-distributed transactions for various reasons such as:

- Some recovery managers are designed to write the objects to the recovery file early-under the assumption that transactions normally commit.

- If transactions use a large number of big objects, the need to write them contiguously to the recovery file may complicate the design of a server. When objects are reference intentions lists, they can be found wherever they are.

- In timestamp ordering concurrence control, a server sometimes knows that a transaction will eventually be able to commit and acknowledges the client at this time the objects are written to the recovery file to ensure their permanency feature. However, the transaction may have to wait to commit until earlier transactions have committed. In such situations, the corresponding transaction status entries in the recovery file will be waiting to commit and then committed to ensure timestamp ordering of committed transactions in the recovery file. On recovery waiting-to-commit transactions can be allowed to commit, because the ones they were waiting for have either just committed or if not have to be aborted due to failure of the server.

Test Your Progress

1. Define:
   i. Transaction recovery
   ii. Checkpoint
   iii. Shadow version

2. What do you mean by log–file? Also explain that how it is used in recovery?

12.7 Summary

In this Chapter, you have learnt about distributed system Distributed transaction maintains the atomicities of all data object stored at different servers and maintain consistency of transaction. All transaction must be maintaining atomicity, they ask to commit the transaction to all participants or abort. They also make log files to recover data objects if server crashes or any other catastrophe may occur during transaction processing.

12.8 Key Terms

- **Edge chasing:** A distributed approach to deadlock detection.
- **IP address:** A numerical label assigned to each device participating in a computer network that uses it for communication.
- **Probes:** The servers which attempt to find cycles by forwarding message.

12.9 Exercise

1. Discuss flat and nested distributed transactions.
2. In the two phase commit protocol, why can be blocking be completely eliminated even when the participants elect a new coordinator?
3. Explain how the two – phase commit protocol for nested transaction ensures that if the top – level transaction commit all the right descendent are committed or aborted.
4. Explain the two – phase commit protocol for nested transactions.
5. How does the distributed deadlock affect the transaction?
6. Define Phantom deadlock.
7. What do you mean by recovery of the two – phase commit protocol?

Chapter 13
Replication

13.1 Introduction

In the previous Chapter, you have learnt about distributed transactions. In this Chapter you will learn about replication. In the distributed database system, the transaction process is present in the form of partitioned database. The database is present at each and every site. If a site in the system is not working well, then its database cannot be accessible by other sites in the system. If the processes on the other sites require the use of a process and that site is not accessible then all such transactions are immediately blocked. This blocking creates a problem in executing the transactions. In this situation, the availability of files can be increased by making the duplicates of the files. By this method, the same file is stored at two or more sites and makes the availability of files easy on the distributed system if anyone site fails down. The copies of a file stored at different sites are called replicas.

Motivations for Replication

The motivations for replication are to improve services performance to increase its availability or to make it fault tolerant.

1. **Performance Enhancement:** Single server acts as a bottleneck. We can balance load among multiple servers, get apparent performance gain. The caching of data at clients end and servers end is by now familiar as a means of performance enhancement.

2. **Increased Availability:** Users require services to be highly available. That is, the proportion of time for which the service or resources is accessible with minimum response times should be close to 100 per cent. Apart from delays, the factors that are relevant to high availability are:

   (a) Server failures
   (b) Network partitions and disconnected operation

   If each of n servers has an independent probability p of failing or becoming unreachable, then the availability of an object stored at each of these servers is:

   $$1 - \text{Probability (all managers unreachable or failed)} = 1 - p^n$$

3. **Fault Tolerance:** Highly available data is not necessarily and strictly correct data. It may be out of date. A fault tolerant service always makes guarantees that strictly correct behaviour must be maintained despite a certain number and type of faults.

The same basic technique used for high availability of replicating data and functionality between computers is also applicable for achieving fault tolerance. If up to n of n + 1 server's crash, then in principle is that at least one remains to supply the service. And if up to n servers can exhibit Byzantine failures, then by the principle a group of 2n + 1 servers can provide correct service, by having the correct servers outvote the failed servers.

When data are replicated the replication transparency is required. That is, clients should not generally have to be aware that multiple copies of data exist at different servers. The other requirement for replicated data is consistency. These concerns whether the operations performed upon a replicated object, the produced results must meet the specification of correctness for those objects.

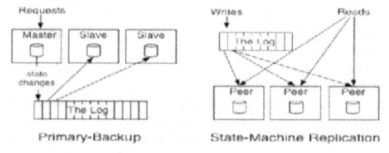

Figure 13.1: Example of Replication

There are some other reasons to replicate system:

1. Replication improves reliability. If data is lost or corrupted due to a system failure, one can use the replica.

2. Replication improves performance. More processors and local memory can be added to the system.

3. Replication saves in communication. When system expands geographically, it is natural to use replicas.

4. Caching is used to improve the efficiency of memory access.

The difficulty of replicas and caching is how to keep the system consistent. All parts of the system should only use the current copy of data, not old one. When new data are stored, how quickly should the replicas be updated?

If tight consistency is required, i.e., all data must be updated in all replicas, it may be very costly and more work may be lost for achieving consistency than what was saved by replication.

Test Your Progress

1. What do you mean by replication?
2. What is the motivation for replication?
3. Why is caching used?

13.2 System Model and Group Communication

The data consists of collection of terms that's called *objects*. But each such logical object is implemented by a collection of physical copies called *replicas*.

System Model: Here, we assume an asynchronous system is which processes fail may only by crashing and network partitions may not occur. For the sake of generality, we describe architectural components by their roles and do not mean to imply that they are necessarily implemented by distinct processes.

The model involves replicas held by distinct replica manager, which are components that contain the replicas on a given computer and perform operations upon them directly. This general model may be applied in a client/server environment, in which a replica manager is a server. It may be applied to an application and application processes can in that case act as both clients and replica managers.

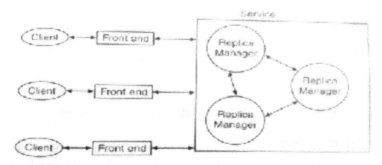

Figure 13.2: Management of Replica Manager

The system model provides for manages replicas and describes group communication.

The model involves replicas cells by distinct replicas managers which are the components that contain the replicas on a given computer and perform operations upon them directly as shown in Figure 13.2.

A full implementation of group communication incorporates a group membership service to manage the dynamic membership of groups in addition to multicast communication. Multicast and group membership management are strongly interrelated. The group communication service has to manage chance in the group's membership while casts take place concurrently.

A group membership service has four main task places concurrently.
1. Providing an interface group membership changes.
2. Implementation of a failure detector.
3. Notifying members of group membership changes.
4. Performing group address expansion.

A full group membership service maintains group views, which are lists of the current group membership identified by their unique process identifiers, the list of ordered according to the sequence in which the members joined group. A new group view is generated when processes are added or executed.

The membership service excludes process from even though it may not have crashed because a communication failure may have made the process unreachable while it continues to excite normally the effect of exclusion is that no message will be delivered to that process hence froth. A false suspicion of a process and consequent exclusion of the process from group may reduce group's effectiveness.

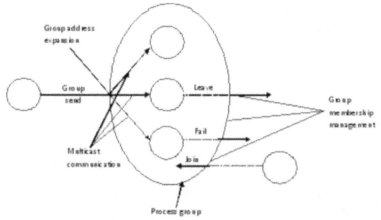

Figure 13.3: Services provided for Process Groups

Group Communications

Group communication occurs when one source process sending amessage to a group of process. Destination is group rather than a single process:

i.   **Broadcast-** destination is everybody.

ii.   **Multicast-** destination is a designated group.

iii. **Unicast-** destination is a single process

A group is a collection of processes: = {p1, p2...p3}

Example of Use

1. **Fault tolerance based on replicated servers:** The service is implemented by a group of server processes. A client sends multicast (send to many) request message to the server group. Each group member performs identical operation on a request.

2. **Locating objects in distributed service:** A distributed file service is implemented by a group of servers. The files are not replicated. A client looking for a particular files multicast the request messages to the server group. The member holds the wanted file responds

3. **Updating replicated data:** Data may be replicated on multiple servers which forms a server group. Update requests are multicasts to the group.

4. **Multiple notifications:** A group of processes need to be notified of certain events. When the event occurs, a message can be multicasted to the group. A specific example of multiple notifications is the multicasting of flight information

to a group of display processes in a airport terminal system.

Test Your Progress

1. Define system model.
2. What do you mean by group communication?
3. Explain the term view delivery.
4. What is the role of group membership service?
5. Explain view-synchronous group communication.

13.3 Fault Tolerant Services

For fault tolerant services, a service is provided that is corrected despite up to process failure by replicating data and functionality at replica managers. For the sake of simplicity we assume that communication remains reliable and no positions occur. Each replica managers is assumed to behave according to the specification at the semantics of the objects it manages, when they do not crash.

For example, a bank account specification would include an assurance that fund transformed between accounts can never disappear and that only deposits and withdraws affect the balance at any particular account.

13.3.1 Passive Replication

In passive model of replication for fault tolerance there is at any one time a single primary replica manager and one or more secondary replica managers backup or salvers. In pure form of model front ends commutate only with primary replica managers to obtain service. The primary replica manager executes operations and sends copies of updated data to backups. If primary fails one of the backups is promoted to act as the primary replica manager.

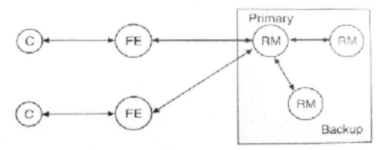

Figure 13.4: Passive Model for Fault Tolerance

Figure 13.4 illustrates a basic architectural model for the management of replication data in which C represents Client, FE represents Front ends and RM represents replica managers.

The sequence of events when a client requests an operation to be performed is as follows:

1. **Request:** The front end sends the request, containing a unique identifier ID, to

the primary replica manager.

2. **Coordination:** The primary replica manager takes each request atomically, in the order in which primary replica receives it. It checks the unique identifier ID, in case if it has already executed the request then it simply re-sends the response.

3. **Execution:** The primary replica manager executes the request and stores the response.

4. **Agreement:** If the request is an update then the primary replica sends the updated state to other replicas or backups, the response and the unique identifier to all the backups. The backups send an acknowledgement to the primary replica.

5. **Response:** The primary replica responds to the front end, which sends the response back to the client.

    Passive replication has the disadvantage of providing relatively large overheads.

13.3.2 Active Replication

Definition: In active mode replication for fault tolerance the replica managers are state machines that play equivalent roles and are organized as a group. Front ends multicast their request to the group of replica managers and all the replica manager process the request independently, but identically and reply. If any replica manager crashes, then it has no impact on the performance of service since the remaining replica manager continues to respond in a normal way.

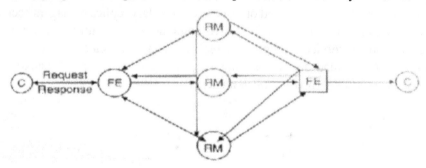

Figure 13.5: Active Replication

Figure 13.5 illustrates the failure management technique managed by active replication. If replica fails, then remove it from the group. Ensure group communication can lose member in middle of communication/computation.

Under active replication, the sequence of events when a client requests for an operation to be performed:

1. **Request:** The Front end always attaches a unique identifier with the request and multicasts it to the group of replica managers (Active replicas), using a totally ordered, reliable multicast primitive. The front end is assumed to fail by crashing at worst case scenario. It does not issue the next request until it has received a response from all replica managers.

2. **Coordination:** It must be ensure that group communication system sends the

request to every correct replica manager in the same order.

3. **Execution:** When requests received then every replica manager executes the request. Because they are state machines and requests are sends in the same order, correct replica managers process the request identically and response contains the client's unique request identifier. When received then we identify correct response by the 'solution of Byzantine failures'.

4. **Agreement:** Here, agreement phase is not required, because of the requests multicast delivery semantics.

5. **Response:** Each replica manager delivers its response to the front end. The number of replies that the front end received depends upon the failure assumptions and multicast algorithm. In this model, system does not reach linearizability. This is because the total order in which the replica manager executes the requests is not sure the same as the real-time order in which the clients are made their requests.

Test Your Progress

1. Describe fault–tolerant services.
2. What do you mean by active and passive replication?

13.4 Highly Available Services

Replication technique is used to make services highly available, i.e., clients access the services with reasonable response time. The several systems they provide the highly available services are:

1. Gossip Architecture
2. Coda File System

Let us discuss each of them in brief.

13.4.1 Gossip Architecture

The gossip architecture is a framework for making highly available service implementations through use of replication. It has been applied to distributed garbage detection and deadlock detection to create a highly available electronic mail service or bulletin board service. The Front ends normally communicate with only a single replica manager at a time all though they are free to communicate with other as shown in Figure 13.6

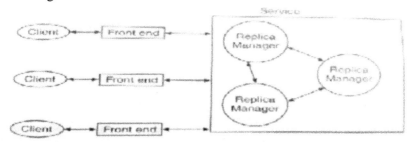

Figure 13.6: Clients communicate with Replica Manager

The replica managers update one another by exchanging gossip messages which contain the most recent update they have received. They are said to update one another in a lazy fashion in that gossip messages may be exchanged only occasionally, after several updates have been collected or when a replica manager finds out that it is missing an update sent to one of its peers, which it needs to process a request.

Figure 13.7 illustrates the event sequence occurred in gossip architecture. There is a relaxed consistency between replicas. All replicas eventually receive all updates. In Figure 13.7 the vector timestamp represents those updates that have been accepted by replica manager, i.e., placed in the manager's log.

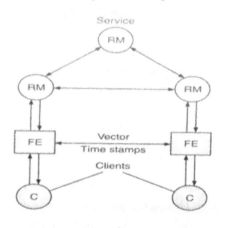

Figure 13.7: Front End Propagate their Timestamps whenever Client communicate Directly

The gossip architecture is aimed at achieving high availability for services. High availability can only be achieved if updates are propagated to more than one failure independent computer in a timely fashion. As the number of replica managers grows, so does the size of the timestamps used and the number of gossip messages that have to be transmitted. If a client makes a query then normally two messages are produced. One approach is to make services scalable and also to make most of the replicas read only. In other words, these replicas are updated by gossip messages but do not receive updates directly from front ends. This arrangement is potentially useful where the update/query ratio is small. Read only replicas can be situated close to clients groups, and update can be serviced by relatively few central replica managers. Gossip traffic is reduced since read only replicas have no gossip to propagate. And vector timestamps need only contain for the replicas that are able to update.

Figure 13.8 illustrates the gossip replica manager internals, i.e., main state components of replication. In this Figure, the tasks performed by replica manager while receiving a gossip message:

● To merge the arriving log with its own.
● To apply updates those have not been executed earlier and also have become stable in nature.
● To reduce records from the log and entries.
● To clear redundant entries from the log.

The function of replica timestamp as shown in Figure 13.8 to represent those updates that have been acknowledged by the replica manager, i.e., placed in the manager's log.

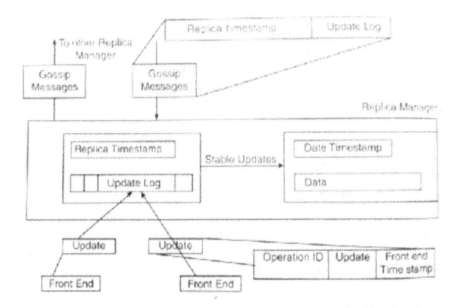

Figure 13.8: Gossip Replica Manager Internals

13.4.2 Coda File System

The Coda file system is a descendent of AFS (Andrew File System) that aims to address several requirements that AFS does not meet, particularly the requirement to provide high availability despite disconnected operation. It has been developed in a research project undertaken Satyanarayanan and his co-workers at Carnegie-Mellon University (CMU). The design requirements for Coda were derived from experience with AFS at CMU and elsewhere involving its use in large scale distributed systems on both local and wide area communication networks.

Coda was designed to be a scalable, secure and highly available distributed file system. An important goal was to achieve a high degree of naming and location transparency so that the system would appear to its users very similar to a pure local file system.

Coda aims to provide users with the benefits of a shared file repository but to allow them to rely entirely on local resources when the repository is partially or totally inaccessible. In addition to these aims, Coda retains the original goals of AFS with regard to scalability and the emulation of UNIX file semantics.

In contrast to AFS, where read-write volumes are stored on just one server, the design of Coda relies on the replication of file volumes to achieve a higher throughput of file access operations and a greater degree of fault tolerance. In addition, Coda relies on an extension of the mechanism used in AFS for caching copies of files at client computers to enable those computers to operate when they are not connected to the network.

Coda Architecture: Coda runs what it calls '*Venus*' processes at the client computers and '*Vice*' processes at file server computers, adopting the AFS terminology. The Vice processes are what we have called replica managers. The Venus processes are the hybrid of from ends and replica managers. They play the front end's role of hiding the service implementation from local client processes; but, since they manage a local cache of files, they are also replica managers, although of a different type to the Vice processes.

The set of servers holding replicas of a file volume is known as the *Volume Storage Group* (VSG). At any instant, a client wishing to open a file in such a volume can access some subset of the VSG, known as the *Available Volume Storage Group* (AVSG). The membership of the AVSG varies as servers become accessible or are made inaccessible by network or server failures.

Normally, Coda file access proceeds in a similar manner to AFS, with cached copies of files being supplied to the client computers by any one of the servers in the current AVSG. As in AFS, clients arc notified of changes via a *callback promise* mechanism but this now depends on an additional mechanism for the distribution of updates to each replica. On close, copies of modified files are broadcasted in parallel to all of the servers in the AVSG.

It is a principle of the design of Coda that the copies of files residing on servers are more reliable than those residing in the caches of client computers.

Coda's replication strategy is optimistic. It allows modification of files to proceed when the network is partitioned or during disconnected operation. It relies on the attachment to each version of a file of a Coda Version Vector (CVV). A CVV is a vector timestamp with one element for each server in the relevant VSG.

In summary, compared with AFS, Coda enhances availability both by the replication of files across servers and by the ability of clients to operate entirely out of their caches.

Test Your Progress

1.   Explain highly available service.
2.   Explain gossip architecture.
3.   Explain query and update operations in a gossip service with suitable example.

13.5 Transaction with Replicated Data

The following are the functioning of system for operating condition and failure during recovery:

1.   **User Transaction:** When a user need to work with a database and make request to read or write the data, since checks for the presence of data at that site. If the data is not found at that site, then the request is rejected by the site. If the data is present at that site, then the request is processed at that site, if data is readable, and if data is found unreadable that copier transaction is initiated for read operation at that site. The copier transaction uses the content of the readable copy to remove the local copy of data. In this way, the local copy becomes readable.

2. **Copier Transaction:** When the site is in recovery state, the copier transaction initiate for the entire data object which are marked as unreadable. Also the copier transaction may be initiated for an individual data object which is found unreadable. The concurrency control which is used by the RDBMS (Relational Database Management System) is also followed by copier transaction.

3. **Control Transaction:** These are the transactions which update all the replicas at different site. Let there is recovery site 'S' which changes its state towards operational state then it chooses the **type 1** control transaction. The **type 1** control transaction reads the missed update process say P from any other site 'K' and then refreshes it at the recovering site 'S'. After this control transaction gives a new session number to that recovery site. If a site is found in the network in one or more sites but in down state, then the **type 2** control transaction is used. Control transaction is also used the concurrency control algorithm for RDBMS by the copier transaction.

> **Note:** *Transaction is sequence of one or more operations applied in such a way as to in enforce the ACID properties.*

13.5.1 Architecture for Replicated Transaction

We assume that a front end sends client requests to one of the group of the replica managers of logical objects. In the primary copy approach, all front ends communicate with a distinguished primary replica manager to perform an operation and that replica manager keeps the backups up-to-date. Alternatively front ends may communicate with nay replica manager to perform an operation but coordination between the replica managers is consequently more complex.

The replica manager that receives a request to perform an operation on a particular object is responsible for getting the cooperation of the other replica managers in the group that have copies of that objects. For example, in the read one/write all scheme, a read request can be performed by a single replica manager, whereas a write request must be performed by all the replica manager in the group that have copies of that project. For example, in the read one/write all scheme a read request can be performed by the entire replica manager in the group.

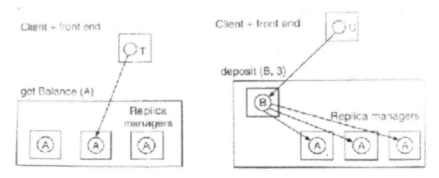

Figure 13.9: Transaction on Replicated Data

Figure 13.9 illustrates replicated transactional service in which each replica manager provides concurrency control and recovery of its own data items in the same way as it does for non-replicated. This approach follows replication schemes which refer a scheme that can also handle network partitions. This scheme is also useful in Quorum consensus and virtual partition. Network partitions separate replica managers into two or more subgroups in which the members of a subgroup can communicate with one another but members of different subgroups cannot communicate.

13.5.2 Available Copies Replication

The available copies scheme is designed to allow for some replica managers being temporarily unavailable. The strategy is that a client reads request on a logical object may be performed by any available replica manager but that a client updates request must be performed by all available replica managers in the group with copies of the object.

In the normal case, client requests are received and performed by a functioning replica manager. Read request can be performed by the replica manager that receives them. Write request are performed by the receiving replica manager and the other entire available replica manager in the group. For example, in Figure 13.10, the get balance operation of transaction T is performed by X, whereas its deposit operation is performed by M, N and P. Concurrent control at each replica manager affects the operation performed locally.

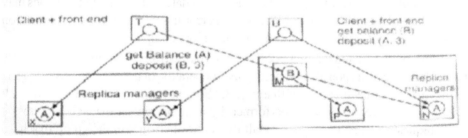

Figure 13.10: Available Copies

Test Your Progress

1. What do you understand by transaction with replicated data?
2. Explain the concept of available copies replication.

13.6 Summary

In this Chapter, you have learnt about the concept of replication. Replication mechanism is used to maintain the availability of data or objects. It also used to handle fault tolerance in distributed system. When a fault occurs in distributed system then replica manager provides a correct data to the server, which requires performing the current transaction or operation.

13.7 Key Terms

- **AVSG**: Available Volume Storage Group.
- **Copier transaction**: A type of transaction which initiates for the entire data object to be marked as unreadable when the site is in recovery state.
- **Gossip architecture**: A framework for making highly available service implementation through use of replication.
- **Objects:** Data consists of collection of terms.
- **Unicast:** A term used to describe communication where a piece of information is sent from one point to another point.

13.8 Exercise

1. Define group communication.
2. What are the main roles of group membership services?
3. Write short notes on:
   i. Gossip architecture
   ii. Coda file system
4. Explain primary replication and Active replication in details.

Practice with Ease for Examination

1. Describe how a non – recoverable situation could arise if write locks are released after the last operation of a transaction but before its commitment. (2006-07)

   Ans: See Section 11.4

2. What are the advantages and drawbacks of multiversion timestamp ordering in comparision with the ordinary timestamp ordering? (2006 -07)

   Ans: See Section 11.6

3. Explain the difference between linearizability and sequential consistency and why the latter is more practical to implement in general? (2006-07)

   Ans: See Section 12.2

4. The two-phase commit protocol is a centralized protocol where the decision to abort or commit is taken by the coordinator. Design a decentralized two-phase commit protocol where no site is designated to be a coordinator. (2007-08)

   Ans: See Section 12.3

5. Describe how a non-recoverable situation could arise if write locks are released after the last operation of a transaction but before its commitment.

   (2007-08, 2012-13)

   Ans: See Section 12.6

6. Explain how the two-phase commit protocol for nested transaction ensures that if the top-level transaction commits all the right descendent are committed or aborted? (2007-08, 2008-09)

Ans: see Section 12.3.1

7. What are commit protocols? Explain how two – phase commit protocols respond to failure of participating site and failure of coordinator?   (2008-09)

    Ans: See Section 12.3.1

8. Explain why serial equivalence requires that once a transaction has released a lock on an object, it is not allowed to obtain any more looks.

    A server manages the objects a_1, a_2, a_3... a_n. The server provides two operations for its clients:

    read (i) returns the value of a_i

    write (i, value) assigns value to a_i

    The transaction T and U defined as follows:

    T: x = read (i); write (j,44);

    U: Write (i, 55); write (j, 66);

    Describe an interleaving of the transaction T and U in which locks are released early with the effect that the interleaving is not serially equivalent. (2008-09)

    Ans: See Section 11.4

9. What are locks? What are essential differences in the lock-based protocols and timestamp based protocols?   (2008-09)

    Ans: See Section 11.4

10. What do you mean by two-phase locking? How it is different from strict two-phase locking? Explain.   (2009-10)

    Ans: See Section 11.4.1

11. Explain the following: (2009-10)

    i.   Fault tolerant services

    ii.   Highly available services

    Ans: See Sections 13.3 and 13.4

12. Explain optimistic concurrency control.   (2011-12)

    Ans: See Section 11.5

13. Explain timestamp ordering for transaction management.   (2011-12)

    Ans: See Section 11.6

14. Explain transactions with replicated data.   (2011-12)

    Ans: See Section 13.5

15. Briefly explain the objective of distributed transaction management. (2012-13)

    Ans: See Section 12.1

16. What is lock? Describe the function of lock manager.   (2012-13)

    Ans: See Section 11.4

17. Draw a schematic diagram of the distributed transaction management model. Explain each component in brief.   (2012-13)

Ans: See Section 12.1

18. Define and differentiate simple and nested distributed transactions. (2012-13)

    Ans: See Section 12.2

19. What is atomic commit protocol? Explain in brief. (2012-13)

    Ans: See Section 12.3

20. Describe the advantages and disadvantages of multiversion timestamp ordering over the ordinary timestamp ordering. (2013-14)

    Ans: See Section 11.6

21. Describe the optimistic concurrency control method. How this method avoids the drawbacks of locking? Explain. (2013-14)

    Ans: See Section 12.4.3

References

1. Singhal & Shivaratri, "Advanced Concept in Operating Systems", McGraw Hill

2. Ramakrishna, Gehrke," Database Management Systems", Mc Grawhill

3. Coulouris, Dollimore, Kindberg, "Distributed System: Concepts and Design", Pearson Education

4. Tenanuanbaum, Steen," Distributed Systems", PHI

5. Gerald Tel, "Distributed Algorithms", Cambridge University Press